2012:

A

SHAM

ODYSSEY

JOHN MOORE

Published 2015, in Great Britain.
Text Copyright © John Moore 2015

ISBN: 978-1517676452

British Cataloguing Publication data:
A catalogue record of this book is available from the British Library

CONTENTS

Contents _____ iii

Introduction _____ 1

Part 1: Sportingly Pursuing Politics and Politics as a Sporting Pursuit _____ 9

Politics at the Olympic Games _____ 18

The Shards of the Spectrum _____ 52

Part 2: Attacking London _____ 89

Poster Children _____ 90

A Class Apart _____ 103

The Athlete's Global Village _____ 115

Part 3: The Multicultural Agenda in Action ___ 132

The Internationalist Influence _____ 133

Fast Girls, Loose Messages _____ 157

The Shambles of Sport and Politics Combining_ 165

Standing on Ceremony - London's Opening and Closing Gambits Reassessed _____ 181

Conclusion: Laying the Foundation for the Future _____ 218

Footnotes: _____ 241

Bibliography: _____ 245

Webography: _____ 248

About The Author _____ 249

CONTENTS

Contents _____ iii

Introduction _____ 1

Part 1: Sportingly Pursuing Politics and Politics as
a Sporting Pursuit _____ 9
   Politics at the Olympic Games _____ 18
   The Shards of the Spectrum _____ 52

Part 2: Attacking London _____ 89
   Poster Children _____ 90
   A Class Apart _____ 103
   The Athlete's Global Village _____ 115

Part 3: The Multicultural Agenda in Action ___ 132
   The Internationalist Influence _____ 133
   Fast Girls, Loose Messages _____ 157
   The Shambles of Sport and Politics Combining_ 165
   Standing on Ceremony - London's Opening and
   Closing Gambits Reassessed _____ 181

Conclusion: Laying the Foundation for the Future
_____ 218

Footnotes: _____ 241

Bibliography: _____ 245

Webography: _____ 248

About The Author _____ 249

INTRODUCTION

"The spirit of these games will inspire a
generation. When our time came, Britain, we
did it right."

With these words, Sebastian Coe brought the curtain down on the 2012 London Olympics; something that, within the pages of this work, I hope to explore and re-analyse as being a grotesque spectacle of unbridled propaganda propped up by brands of nationalism and patriotism at their least authentic. More specifically, they were so much more than a mere two week sporting spectacle of various amateurs partaking in various sporting disciplines few have anything to do with for the time in-between hastily gathering round a television set once every four years to see who wins. Moreover, it is my intension to explore here an idea that the Games were, in actual fact, a meticulously planned and devilishly executed social engineering project designed to shake the nation of Great Britain and its populous to its very core. It would do this through a very specific coded political hypothesis, the likes of which had their roots in the reformist attitudes of the liberal political elite who in one authors eyes, had already, at least culturally, [1]"...been in power for years".

When Coe addressed a salivating multi-racial; multi-cultural Britain with the above, he did so to conclude a deeply contorted two week exhibition of a very particular brand of civic nationalism further still within in a locale that had become very different to the one which last hosted the Games. The "we" of the remark were neither the athletes nor the organisers. Nor were they even the citizens. They were the politicians and the officials responsible for the whole spectacle; those who gave it its life at the very beginning early on in the decade of the 2000's right up to those who had a hand in directing its closing ceremony. This was a mixture of Labour and Conservative personalities, those of whom were of a very specific generation and of whom shared a deeply personal body of politic more broadly orientated to reforming Britain's institutions and its identity. Vital to the overall argument contained within is the point that, while the Olympic project was hatched and nurtured under the tutelage of Tony Blair and his New Labour engine, it was formally delivered by the post 2010 Coalition of David Cameron and his Liberal partners. At its core was a one-time Conservative Member of Parliament, in Sebastian Coe.

The "we" in the speech were thus the politicians behind the entire escapade, not the people in the auditorium who had delivered the Games in the first place with their partaking in it or aiding in volunteering; nor too was it those sitting at home in front of their televisions whose interest and viewing figures proved the International Olympic Committee were correct in awarding the Games to a sport-interested Britain in the first place. The reason for this was that they had successfully manoeuvred their way around numerous barriers, some not entirely within the boundaries of their control, in order to create a sporting spectacle so distinct in its political nature that it would come to inspire a generation to embrace the ideologies promoted by the Games themselves.

It must thus be noted that, beginning in 2004 with the bid itself under the watchful eye of Labour, at no point did the *vision* of these Olympics actually change in any evident capacity in terms of its bare-boned dynamic up until its delivery eight years later. This is in spite of the shift in political power from one of the three main parties to the other two during this time.

Said vision, coined by Blair and later provided by Cameron, was undoubtedly to revel in Britain's post-war shift in identity: to be able to doff one's cap to that of where immigration has led us; to encourage a nation of multiple faiths vying with one another for supremacy, but confused as to whether they could tread on one another's toes too much, and to inspire youngsters to utilise all of their efforts and energies to invest in newfound heroes of whom were black, white, half-caste, Muslim, homosexual and sometimes a combination of two or more of these.

I hope to demonstrate that the Games themselves were designed to be a celebration of what Britain was, not how good it was in any kind of sporting capacity. These Games, the likes of which were entrenched in the political like so many others as I will come to explore, were, in effect, the lab experiment of post-1960's cultural revolutionaries, whose bodies may have matured over time but whose minds; attitudes and philosophies largely remained the same. They were initiated by people very much a part of New Labour's party of stealth revolution from 1997 and onwards, and did not move in any way as to its core makeup by a party, in the Conservatives, supposed to be all about tradition and remaining entrenched in their fondness for all things old fashioned when the chance came to do such a thing in 2010.

By the end of 2012, and through these games specifically, the Conservative Party would have, for many, officially dropped a ball which in the eyes of some had already long ago hit the ground. To others of less insight, this would have been that moment: when a one-time patriotic athlete himself, and former Commons representative, refused to distance himself from a spectacle of politics and propaganda wherein the dangers of Islam in one's country were blanketed with athletes doing funny arm gestures; wherein the poster child of the whole experiment was female and caught between being black and Caucasian; where it was aggressively put across that traditional gender roles count for nothing, since women can now be boxers and men are pretty good at gymnastics.

Henceforth, I will channel effort into proposing that the 2012 Summer Olympics were but a mere smoke screen: designed to mask several fundamental problems with contemporary Britain and the society it finds itself encompassing, characterised by numerous things ranging from the crisis of identity it is undoubtedly suffering to the creeping shift of the ethnic makeup of its major cities.

When Lord Coe spoke of the "spirit" of the Games inspiring a generation, he was not speaking in ethical terms – it was not a suggestion that the 'get up and go' attitude quite clearly inherent in our athlete's determination to win medals would transfer onto the rest of the population. The jobless will remain jobless due to large scale deindustrialisation in the 1980's and more recent attitudes towards immigration – two things no political party with any realistic aspirations of winning recognition have any desire to combat. The 'together-as-one' mentality epitomised in how the volunteers bravely grouped together to bring the Games to life will do nothing to contribute to breaking down the walls built up by multiculturalist sectioning, and nor will the well-organised security of the event transpose into the nation's lawless, un-policed streets.

Moreover, the spirit of these games was more of a *visual* thing – it was something you could watch and observe. Shamefully, it was in the colour of a competitor's skin; it was in their religion; it lay with the nation of their place of birth; it lay in the fact they were involved in a mixed race relationship, even a mixed race marriage, and had borne children from such a thing. It lay in the potential of somebody's sexual orientation and the inverting of traditional gender roles in society.

Coe's speech to a watching worldwide audience on that warm August evening of 2012 had him reiterated how "we" did it right. What did "we" do right, exactly? Was it that we successfully defended the games from terrorist attacks? That we did well in the medal table? Or perhaps it was that we built the venues in time. What was done correctly was the transplanting of a politic of multiracialism and multiculturalism, epitomised in certain athletes and their apparent supremacy over others, out into the public domain and into young minds as we step evermore dangerously into the wider domestic unknown with our relaxed contemporary laws on everything from policing to immigration to cannabis reform and to homosexual marriage.

Coe, an individual who would likely slip very comfortably into a Labour seat given his lack of enthusiasm to distance himself from an expensive exhibition of politics and strands of what now constitutes as nationalism in the popular eye, is referring to both himself and those who preceded him when he speaks of "our" time. Indeed, it was the time of Blair; of Ken Livingstone; of Tessa Jowell, of Jack Straw and all of the others sharing Blair's ideals that brought us the games during a rigid campaign that essentially began in 2002 and culminated in 2005.

As a result, and by the closing orators own analysis, we have a "generation" of inspired people to look forward to; people whose singular summer all those years ago was spent watching and engaging in a fortnight of sorry propaganda dedicating to raging against all that Britain once was. They would have done this through cheering a Muslim, in Mohamed Farah, to Olympic Gold; through enjoying seeing the tried and traditional turf of Wimbledon trussed up with bright colours and funny logos, likely sharing American tennis star Serena Williams' view that she preferred it this way and will miss it being like this in the future. They would have done this through hearing about centuries old rooms at Lord's Cricket Ground being converted into the sorts of environments totally alien to it, and would have enjoyed hearing leading British cricket correspondent Jonathan Agnew's perplexed reaction during a report from the Long Room that a portrait of W.G. Grace had been covered up in favour of something relevant to the archery there that week. In a more physical sense, the booting out or covering up of the 'old' with the 'new' was undeniable – the raw hatred, in the form of the tennis, of tradition unquestionable.

And in this lies my hypothesis, that London 2012 was a crude; misjudged and entirely worthless two week spectacle built on the diversity and reformism of a very specific set of politicians of a very particular generational stock. Throughout, I will pay reference to a text penned by Mike Lee on the winning of the bid, and how much of what we saw at London in 2012 derived from a very precise series of liberal philosophies utilised and expressed by those in charge of winning its bidding process and executing the Games themselves when the time came. This would range from picking the respective personnel for each of the disciplines to deciding what the opening ceremony might look like. Away from the likes of those who were instrumental in winning the games are both the cultural and historical significances of the London Games; specifically, where they stand in the pantheon of sporting events exploited for political gain and how a number of aspects of the Games, ranging from its base history as a socialist alternative to fighting for right of land under the banner of national flags to the modern architecture of the host city itself, are immensely relevant.

PART 1:
SPORTINGLY PURSUING POLITICS AND POLITICS AS A SPORTING PURSUIT

"Serious sport is war minus the shooting"

George Orwell

"I believe that political correctness can be a form of linguistic fascism, and it sends shivers down the spine of my generation who went to war against fascism."

P.D. James

It adorns its wearer, doing so looking tattered and old. It has seen better days and indeed has never come close to seeing anything quite like what it is going through now. Its owner is a morose looking man, although not due to any internal problem he possesses, but because of what is happening around him on the outside. The item in question is the attire worn by the lead character at a very specific point in 2006 Alfonso Cuaron film *Children of Men*, a specially designed piece of official merchandise clothing with the "official" London 2012 emblem on it as well as the accompanying host city and year. The film itself is a gruelling science fiction, set in a Great Britain in the year 2027 which further-still finds itself in a world in total disarray out of the human race's odd sudden inability to reproduce.

The presence of the garment seemed like a curious aside when first viewing the film nearer to its time of being released than to the 2012 Olympics themselves, even an irrelevance - nothing more than an in-joke. But *after* the Games, the film itself looks positively prophetic - an eerie glancing into what might constitute as the future of the country from as far back as the year 2006. With everything in the film unfolding as it does, and with an unspoken preface to the events depicted therein looming over what we are privy to seeing, the inclusion of the jumper looks now like a reminder that when you embrace the very cultural items and codes the London 2012 Olympics both stood for and openly promoted, one should get ready for where it will take you.

The film, at its hairiest and when it is depicting its second unit content, essentially sees its lead scramble their way through a variety of situations which mostly involves shooting; running; escaping and generally doing one's best to stay out of the way of an all-out Civil War. This is due to the fact such a thing is now tearing Britain apart due to the multi-faith-cultural-racial experiment of a generation prior. The film, of course, needs the expansive premise of a global epidemic which will eventually lead to our species' extinction to really propel that distinct feeling of hopelessness and impending destruction. But the atmosphere of despondency and approaching doom therein, however, is already apparent when we glance at what constitutes as a typical London street; already apparent when we realise the remaining people who choose to remain in Britain, out of some rooted hope that things, civically, will pick up and the epidemic will be cured, are forced to live in secluded areas of the countryside.

The sad reality is that years of abusive politics put in place to shake the very foundations of the country of Great Britain will lead to the very visceral *look* of what London embodied twenty years on in *Children of Men* being a reality. In the film, the rising Asian influence on how the city looks has, for instance, seen rickshaws become a popular way to get around. Meanwhile, violent left wing underground cells purporting to be against fascism operate freely, but do so in an equally fascistic and narrow minded way, via bomb threats and street side abductions, in ways not dissimilar to how organisations such as the UAF (Unite Against Fascism) do so in reality in the early years of twenty-first century England.

Otherwise, mind-numbing and time consuming electronic gadgets dominate people's lives; demonstrated in a scene whereby a young man is so preoccupied with the electronic invention he has wired to his fingertips and hooked up to his temples at the dinner table that he barely even looks capable of conversation, never mind anything else. This is much in the same way social media and the allure of retreating to the screen of one's cellular phone does presently. In the film, World War One monuments stand in predominantly immigrant controlled zones hideously defaced with graffiti; the very things the soldiers died for in said war long since passed on and replaced by something else.

This is not unlike how a war monument, dedicated specifically to the efforts made by animals during the *Second* World War, was defaced with the word "Islam" in the aftermath of the 2013 murder of Lee Rigby, and is also reminiscent of how various people swung on the flags belonging to various London war memorials during the tuition fees protests of November 2010. The notion of social decay and a genuine lack of respect for what preceded you are apparent. Meanwhile, metal detectors adorn the entrances to a standard, government run building and steel grills cover train windows to avoid the rocks being hurled by young, thuggish youths breaking through and injuring somebody.

The frightening image of London in *Children of Men*, a film depicting a Britain essentially living in the afterglow of the Olympics, and given what we know they represented, has not boded well for the city and the nation to which it belongs.

More broadly, my work here is both an exploration and an attack of the London 2012 Summer Olympics as we saw it and as we knew it; a deconstruction of that [1]"...incredible 16 days of Olympic action" in 2012 as July crossed into August and how it was, more broadly, a complete fake designed to titillate Leftists and multiculturalists of this once great nation whilst more broadly shun the right in its hapless attempts at rebranding what nationalism really is.

The question needs to be asked as to how it came to be that a coalition of aggressive Left wingers; Blairites; former socialists; New Labour pioneers and one particular London Mayor who had [2]"never been an avid sports fan" came to join together in bringing a festival of sport and flag waving to a city which was once the indomitable headquarters of a nation who ran most of the world. How they managed to do it was through the importance of Sebastian Coe's bid thesis; notions of economic regeneration and the idea of a legacy of diversity which looked to the future and hoped to provide inspirational figures for what was, on the surface, a worldwide audience but pertained more to those watching at home as children and adults alike cheered on their favourite athletes.

What is to be explored within these pages is, tersely, as to how a twenty-six year old half-caste woman became the "face" of the games and whether it would at all have been possible for someone of the same age and gender to have attained said mantle had they been of a white disposition. Furthermore, it needs to be asked as to whether it was a coincidence that the leading names and personalities of the games, both before; during and after, each consisted of this same half-caste personality; a Muslim long distance runner and a homosexual diver.

For too often the idea of sport and politics clashing, hideously and erroneously, has been linked to dictatorships or political premierships with a distinctly amoral reputation and a penchant for chaos and murder. This may be true for something like Adolf Hitler's 1936 Berlin Games, but it is worth exploring as to how a political premiership with the sort of free and polished surface New Labour had could too be responsible for a deeply political and highly charged sporting spectacle related to the Olympic Games and buried in the hatred of something else.

Indeed, my ultimate hypothesis here is that London 2012 was the equivalent of the Berlin 1936 games, only the *reverse*. At the core of either of them was the unquenchable desire to prove that something ideological could function properly and supremely, rendering those who spoke out against it outdated and wrong. Respectively, either of these political elements were white, Germanic Aryan supremacy and "British" multi-racial multiculturalism. The questions at the forefront of Adolf Hitler's Berlin exhibition were as to whether a white, Aryan race, whose very existence saw its basis draw inspiration from the mythical Nordic bloodline fantasy of a supreme warrior conquering and pillaging its enemies, could prove themselves as physically superior to all that the word threw at them - with particular attention to the Jews and Slavs of Eastern Europe and the Negro of the United States.

Fast forward to 2012 and you have an Olympiad taking place under a similarly highly politicised umbrella, although looking to prove the opposite: was it at all possible for a nation openly proud of its make-up of blacks; whites; half-castes; Christians; Muslims and both hetero and homosexual personnel to stand as one and get behind a squad consisting of most of the above? Could it be that this was the moment that it was proved that various people of each of these different backgrounds and cultures could come together as one and compete for Britain with pride?

Ah, but I hear you scoffing at what I have to say; dismissing it as falsehood or conspiracy. How could something that was so obviously apolitical as the 2012 London Olympics, a mere sporting event whose turn to host it in 2012 just happened to be ours, and of which was little more than something which brought everyone together through their television sets and casual conversations, be so drenched in something nobody else seems to think was apparent? Why should something so embedded within the realm of politics be so synonymous with two weeks of good, clean and hard fought sporting contest? How could the process of a fellow human-being watching a fellow human-being harmlessly engaging in the oldest and purest of sporting formats be as wretched and counterfeit as is being stated here?

Indeed, why would a female role model, whose career choice is set away from the live stages of drug addled rock concert performances and nonsensical reality television shows, and is instead out there on the running track, have the potential to be so destructive to a child? How could something so many people cherished and enjoyed be so incredibly toxic?

Quandaries and questions aside, the answer put simply is: "politics". Make no mistake that the London Olympics of 2012 were just as terrible; just as arid and just as dangerous as I maintain they were. This is not a conclusion I have reached out of the economics of the event, as so many had already done prior to the teams even being announced; nor is it a petty criticism I have coined because I was frustrated at the endless hours of television and Internet coverage which may have made way for alternate programming. Nor too does it have anything to do with London's own brief transformation as a city which, for two weeks, busily welcomed in the world but frustratingly stood still for the people who frequent it daily, as public transport was placed under considerable strain and special Olympic road lanes were laid down for those privileged enough to be qualified to use them.

Moreover, this is a conclusion reached out of what was going on in-between all of this – it lies in whom we were being asked to accept and whom we were being asked to rally against. It lay in what we were being asked to believe and what we were being told was no longer any good. Ultimately, it was a conclusion reached in viewing a spectacle that evidently had an expensive and glossy exterior, but was found rotting on the inside. It lay in the politics of the beast, and the politics of the people behind it – it lay in what history can teach us and with the mentalities of the people with the authority to initiate something like the Olympic Games in the first place. It lay with what was going on in Great Britain generally away from the sailing waters; off the running tracks; out of the swimming pools and detached from the badminton courts. It lay in what was inside the minds of those who brought it here and it lay in the physical manifestation of what that was.

POLITICS AT THE OLYMPIC GAMES

"There are some people who still enjoy skiing for fun"

Arnold Lunn, remarking on Nazi Germany's preoccupation with using skiing as a means to prove Aryan supremacy at Garmisch-Partenkirchen 1936.

Try to picture the scene. It is a hot day in the city of Harare, Zimbabwe, in February of 2003. The setting is the Harare Sports Ground, a quaint little cricket stadium in its nation's capital for a match between the hosts and that of England. From up in the stands, or from the commentary position, the grass appears lush and true; specially manicured for this, a World Cup pool match between two teams not expected to do much in the tournament, but both with the modest reckoning that they could get beyond round one. The hosts, one of three along with South Africa and Kenya, have already played one match: a thumping win against part-timers Namibia, so tensions and passions are high going into the fixture against a team everybody likes beating for the fact it is their game and was once their empire.

The crowd is large and boisterous, colour is everywhere; the predominant reds of Zimbabwe's kit adorning the team's fans is in the clear majority yet finds a way to clash with the blue of England's. England themselves are led by Duncan Fletcher, himself a Zimbabwean and veteran of the 1983 tournament when he represented them. Under Fletcher, England have undergone an incredible revival since his 1999 appointment; garnering long sought after test series wins against the West Indies at home in 2000 and a string of impressive performances both home and away that include drawing with India and winning in Pakistan. Here, this is their opening match and they are desperate for a good start against a team they are expected to beat in a group which also contains the Indians and the Australians. Only the top three out of seven can progress to round two.

England are batting and Zimbabwe are bowling. This means Marcus Trescothick is shaping up to take on the first ball and that Nicolas Knight is waiting at the other end. In a few days' time, he will face one of the fastest deliveries ever recorded in a cricket match when the team takes on Pakistan. Trescothick's inception into international cricket has been extraordinary, with runs against most bowlers both home and away in an opening position once-dominated by Michael Atherton at test level for over a decade.

The bowler is Heath Streak, probably the best bowler Zimbabwe have ever produced in their short history as a full time cricketing nation. He holds a white cricket ball in his hands, this being a one day game featuring coloured clothing, and stands at the beginning of his run. The field is just about set; the sun is out; commentators and spectators alike are looking forward to the exhibition and England's world cup is about to get underway, doubly relieving when we recall that the last time they took to the field four years ago in a world cup fixture, they themselves were hosts and embarrassingly exited in the first round on account of not beating Zimbabwe heavily enough in an earlier fixture.

Only, there is a problem: none of the above actually took place. But, why not? Politics. Politics is why not. Politics pollutes sport, pure and simple; it ruins the spectacle and takes away from the viewer a brand of something authentic and engaging. In boycotting the match on the grounds of not agreeing with the politics of then Zimbabwean leader Robert Mugabe, England forfeited the game and handed Zimbabwe the four pool points. As the tournament rolls on, the Indians and the Australians top the group with Zimbabwe third and England just behind in fourth; a measly two points behind in what is a gap that would otherwise have been made up had the match gone ahead.

Everybody else plays Zimbabwe, and those who were expected to win did so - those who were not expected to, fail to. England was thus one of those who failed to, and as a result the makeup of the event was contaminated; the purity of who may have progressed;

may not have progressed and may have had an ultimate say on the outcome of the whole thing were denied due to a combination of sport and politics.

Aside from contaminating the wholesomeness of the tournament itself, the decision was monumentally misjudged on a personal and ethical level, for it is the job of sportsmen not to play politics but to play sports. Similarly, it is not the job of politicians to dip their toes into the world of sports, as we shall see, but to play at politics: the contestants in this sense are their respective political opponents and a designated electorate. Mugabe's Zimbabwe would not have been selected to host a World Cup if the International Cricket Council thought it against an ethical norm, indeed for many decades South Africa were excluded from various cricketing; footballing and rugby based tournaments due to their Apartheid policies. I mention South Africa and cite the concept of racial Apartheid for the simple reason Mugabe's Zimbabwean nightmare of the time resembled such a thing.

The decision for teams, England and everyone else, to play against Zimbabwe were already made in that respect - it was thus up to the players to go ahead and play. The dynamic of having to play Zimbabwe *in* the nation of Zimbabwe was a further, unpleasant complication, but recall that not only were Mugabe's nation not prohibited from playing in the tournament, but they were duly allowed to *play host* to a handful of pool matches much in the same way the Dutch were in 1999 or the French were in the same year's Rugby

World Cup. When players begin to take matters into their own hands, and make the political decisions which have already been made for them, a sense of farce prevails. Let us say, hypothetically, that a member of the New Zealand team, who espouses especially right-wing views, disagrees with what South Africa has become since Nelson Mandela's release and presidential premiership and refused to play them because of the *abolition* of Apartheid.

Let us pontificate further that that same person disagreed with the direction multicultural Australia was heading at around the same time, refusing to play in said nation out of spite at said politics. Perhaps a West Indian hates Islam and boycotts the playing of Pakistan; maybe a Hindu in the Indian team is at odds with how the Sri Lankan government treats its Hindu population and takes issue with having to play against them. These things could be extended to all manner of sports and events involving a variety of political and theological dynamisms; in the process creating chaos as sporting personnel cross the divide into possessing opinions on things beyond who should be in the team and what should happen on a field of play. This was especially evident for a long time over the issue of Israel being a member of the Asian football federation for much of the twentieth century; something which caused many Arab states in its proximity to boycott the occasions they were drawn to play them. As a consequence of this chaos, Israel very nearly qualified for a World Cup without so much as even having to play a game.

Eventually, they were forced out of the federation and succumbed to joining Europe.

In a few months' time, Heath Streak would be back facing England in a Test Match during Zimbabwe's summer tour to England, and would issue a statement about walking off the pitch at Lord's Cricket Ground in London should anti-Mugabe protestors run onto the outfield like they have been threatening to. When this actually comes to pass, early on during day one of a May 2003 test match when Streak himself is bowling, he does nothing and gets on with the game; likely realising how foolish he risks looking should he do it by himself and how disruptive his actions would be in the long run.

A few months previously at the World Cup, this did not stop his fellow teammates Andrew Flower and Henry Olonga from doing what they did at the eleventh hour of being able to do it. More specifically, and during Zimbabwe's opening match of the tournament against Namibia, both men took to the field adorning black armbands; the universal sign in sport signalling the players involved mourning somebody's death, but here designed to signal the death of democracy and decency with regards to how President Robert Mugabe was running their country.

The image was striking if for the fact nobody knew too much as to what was going on insomuch nobody else on the field were wearing armbands. Furthermore, the sight of one white man and one black gentleman sharing what later become obvious as being this political burden added an extra weight of dynamism. Thought had gone into this; a strike at Mugabe's empire had been hatched, planned and executed in a way that was so simplistic yet so effective and all the while at a time and in a place where the man himself could do nothing in the immediate future about it.

The two men paid for it - not with their lives, but with their livelihoods; each of them having had to flee Zimbabwe post-match and never return for fear of reprisals. Their careers as international cricketers were over, regardless of how much they each had left to give. Flower continued to play first class cricket, doing so in England, while Olonga took up commentating and journalism and whose well-spoken tones adorned the airwaves during that summer of 2003 when he flitted between television and radio stints during Zimbabwe's said tour of England. On one occasion, in-between hopping back and forth from these duties, he accidently greeted those listening on the radio with "Hello, viewers" in what was an instance demonstrating real modesty and innocence.

This did not sound like the man who had it in him to take a swipe at Mugabe's regime and then high-tail it out of there as if a character in an espionage novel. Nor too, did it seem, that Flower was quite finished with playing cricket at the very highest level. Alas, politics once again pollutes sport. What people think and feel make their way out onto the pitch and places not only lives in danger but prematurely terminates people's careers. As I hope to explore in this chapter, when the politics of the outside world clash with sporting events that are as widely considered to be as important and world reaching as the Olympics are, the results can be toxic; unnecessary and often explosive. More broadly, we will come to explore as to how the London Games of 2012, through a variety of different people; their beliefs and the personnel involved in the Games themselves, came to represent one of these instances.

Vital to both the theme of this chapter and my work here overall is the assertion that the act of hosting an Olympic Games does *not* qualify a country as any kind of worthwhile locale. The being granted permission to host the two-week spectacular of sporting spectacle that is the Olympic Games does not automatically render you as some kind of all-impressive, all-encompassing realm which is now characteristic of possessing tremendous wealth; prosperity and commendable levels of safety. Indeed, just because London was the hosts of the Olympic Games in 2012 does not mean that it is exempt from both problem and flaw.

In spite of this, and for too long during both the bidding process and the time in-between winning the right to host it and the opening ceremony, it often felt as if the personnel behind the project thought as if it might; as if, with all the reform that has been undertaken, the crowning glory which goes inextricable lengths in proving that our philosophies are the right ones is the fact that we possess the Olympics.

More specifically with regards the first point, and more tersely than perhaps one would like to be, one is able to use two very distinct events from both the preceding and subsequent summer to that of 2012, in the nation-wide scenes of rioting and disturbances and the ritualistic murder of British solider Lee Rigby on a public street in 2011 and 2013 which best epitomise the decay in social and moral standards. Indeed, if there was a delusion that Britain, or more specifically London, was doing well and making tremendous gains in healing the more immediate wounds created because of the 2011 summer disturbances, when the bubble of Fabian reformism was very violently burst, with the spectacle that-was the London Games, then it was very quickly quelled again the *following* summer with the barbaric murder of a soldier in a public street.

It must be affirmed that to be of the opinion that the Games laid to rest the fears that the country was divided and on the brink of gross reformation, due to the strain of mass immigration; preoccupation for devolution; unhealthy domestic fondness for an ideology as poisonous as Islam and on top of a disastrous fiscal situation, which sees too much money go on foreign venture such as European Union membership and wars abroad, would be ridiculous. And yet, this was precisely how the Olympics were sold to an unsuspecting public, who did nothing to resist absorbing every line and morsel the Olympics channelled through its actions on how immigration enriches us; we are better off being in the European Union and that Islam means peace.

Should the above have Britain sound as if it is on the road to absolute ruin, or worse yet to a state completely indistinguishable to that of what it was for hundreds of years, then it would somewhat perversely be in line with the majority of Olympic legacies. The fact remains that there is a tendency for nations in the "modern" era, that is to say after the Berlin Games of 1936, to have hosted the Olympic Games whilst in a state of terrible trouble. That is to say, broken; directionless and on very fleeting occasions, with the potential to erupt into chaos and bloodshed. Hosting the Olympics does not improve lives, nor does it solve the problems of the era that the nation faces. Olympic programmes are not the answer to the issues inherent in people's lives and it does not constitute as a rubber stamping of a place as serene and worthwhile.

In spite of this, the spectacle of the Games themselves, of which we could realistically accept as unspoken rhetoric, too often felt like a suggestion that you should be of the opinion that the Games did precisely this. Indeed, the overall politic of the Games lay in that we should all count ourselves to be very lucky that these various types of Britons all co-exist with one another, and are able to do so in the manner that they do. Accepting London 2012's definition of what made Britain a great place would be foolish, in that it would lie in the believing that having to live alongside Muslims; celebrating socialism and putting one's faith in either multi-racial relationships or the sorts of people whom support such things.

There is a track record of nations proudly hosting the Olympics, often doing so with the arrogance in mind that their ways are superior to all other ways, just as there is a history of undesirable places hosting them. Beginning with the obvious, in Berlin 1936, we observe a dictatorship whose persecution of minorities and eventual desire for some form of worldwide domination saw the movement propelling the whole experiment implode in an inglorious display of bloodshed and raw hatred merely nine years after boasting to having hosted the Games. Moving on from there, we observe London in 1948 still weeping from the strains of wartime life - a nation whose rationing regulations would not cease for several more years and a nation shrouded in an enormous amount of both grief and low morale, as it came to terms with not only the tremendous loss suffered from the last five years, but also the slow realisation that their place in the world as a global power would change insurmountably from now on.

The Mexico City Games of 1968 did not do away with the vile narcotic epidemic which has characterised said nation for so long, whereas the 1972 Games in Munich had little-to-no bearing on whether Germany might become reunited any time in the future; nor too did it have any impact or say on whether the people in the East might ever be free once again from the grotesque forms of Leftism that was polluting that country and which essentially brought rise to the Nazis in the first place. During Munich, Germany itself was a nation cut in half: a country whose capital could not even be crossed but for roadblocks constructed out of ideological hatred - a city whose more typical iconography in this sense invoked that of a prison camp, as people were destined to live out their lives either under the icy grip of he who ran the Soviet Union, or under the more capitalist imbued Americans, whose control and influence on the German way of life for all those years depressingly resonates to this day when we observe the official language of their air force is "American-English".

In 1980 and 2008, two separate nations with Communist leanings hosted the Games; the first of which was the Soviet Union – a nation which, like Nazi Germany, was a dictatorship and not shy of invading its neighbours. It must additionally be noted that, like the Germany of 1936, the Union of Socialist Soviet Republics went from being able to boast of hosting the Olympics to not even existing a mere eleven years later – not unlike Hitler's Germany, which was run into the ground in a few less.

Those who desire life in China must undertake the respective means to make such a transition possible, but they will be doing so in order to move to a nation whose own tendency to persecute Tibetans was so fierce that it made its way onto the streets of London in 2008 as the Olympic flame went on its annual tour prior to the Beijing Games. Put frankly, here again is a nation barely a step away from being a dictatorship; a nation whose own sordid history on a modern domestic front may be set away from a German STASI officer or a

Stalinist social purge, but whose ability to wave a wand of political suppression enables it to strike fear into those within its borders.

We saw this in the aftermath of an incident that occurred in March 2014, when a terrorist attack at a Kunming train station involving knives and Islam (so often a lethal cocktail) saw a lone believer of the said faith, and who was part of a group wrapped up in a complicated body of geo-politics, kill thirty-three people as well as himself in order to make a point to the Chinese government. This was followed up not so long afterwards with further attacks by the same militant group, whose demand for some kind of political recognition within their Xinjiang province were put across in the starkest of ways.

Over the ensuing months, the Chinese government went into lockdown in attempting to keep its high population in order; initiating a series of "anti-terror" measures that saw patrols return to the streets and what was described by some over one of China's leading social media outlets as a hark [3]"...back to the paranoia of a Mao era, where every banal act of attitude could become ammunition", when it was revealed thousands of people were being paid to turn "informer" on those who were behaving or conversing suspiciously.

The report from which the above derives went on to explore these incentives, describing them as being [4]"...calibrated to appeal to Beijing's poor urbanites", allowing those who produce detailed information on what the state want being able to [5]"...earn the provider

20p – the price of a bowl of noodles." It goes on, informing us that [6]"...a category of salaried 'supergrass' will be created, paying £20 a month to those able to provide three nuggets of information every day." Lastly, and perhaps most disturbingly, we are informed of a number of hotel managers outside of Beijing that were sent for [7]"corrective education" for leaving a complimentary box of matches in a hotel suite, such was the newfound allergy to flammables and so forth following the threat of Islamic attacks.

Said attacks came at a particularly unpleasant moment in history, for China itself was about to acknowledge the twenty-fifth anniversary of the Tiananmen Square protest of 1989 – an event the Chinese are, by and large, not even allowed to commemorate anyway, with many-an activist; academic and lawyer having been caught out in the past attempting to do such a thing and punished.

Things became more complicated in September of the same year, when the Chinese government revealed some unpleasant colours pertaining to their apparent hatred of democracy in their suppressing of hundreds of students in Hong Kong over their desire to choose their elected representatives via the voting process. This desire stemmed from an alternative which would instead see China merely hand them representatives down via a selection process. So much for a rich, diverse-laden Beijing 2008 legacy, where not only the shambles of the regime propping China up was exposed mere years later in these examples, but the nature of the country's cultural and theological set up appeared to be at odds with itself.

1984 saw the turn of Los Angeles to, once again, adopt the mantel of host; yet, this aforementioned shining beacon of modern multiculturalism and multiple racialism, with blacks; whites; Hispanics and Koreans all occupying this dense set of neighbourhoods and districts, was practically burnt to the ground eight years after it had had its finest sporting hour, when tensions over how certain ethnic fiefdoms were treated hit boiling point upon the assault of Rodney King. Life in Los Angeles since, as documented in often moving works of cinema *Boyz in the Hood* (1991) and *Falling Down* (1993) have suggested the Utopian reputation the city carries, of movie stars; beautiful people and sports cars, is somewhat different to the multi-cultural melting pot it actually is. What is relevant here is as to how the Olympic Games, and all the money spent on such a project years earlier, did not aid in either the regeneration of said city nor the harmonising of said city's inhabitants with one another.

Likewise, the Greek economy in 2014, precisely ten years after Athens had hosted, suggested that just because a nation obtains the golden chalice of the Olympic Games, does not mean that what they did right in order to obtain such an honour will see them in good fiscal stead for the forthcoming future. This was something Western politicians, and Greeks alike, had to take stock of in January 2015, when an election returned a coalition government committed to an anti-austerity political philosophy. While we are on the subject of Eurozone nations, although here looking at what is being theorised here from the opposite angle, Germany had gone without hosting an Olympic Games since both 1972 and their reunification, yet possessed an economy considerably more stable to that of Greece's at the time.

Beneath the surface majesty of each of these examples of winning the Olympic bid lies an inconvenient truth that the respective nations have largely been either undemocratic; oppressive; struggling with a crisis of identity or culture; treading thin economic lines or just generally unpleasant. There have been exceptions, in the form of a South Korean Olympics and a Canadian one, which passed off with more sobriety than the above, although were not free of a domestic economic moan, but the sad fact is that London 2012 must join the list of Olympic movements which brought to the table more in the form of pain than it did gain, and was executed in such a way that made a lot of us feel as if we did not even matter.

Crucially, we must remember that in amongst all of this, politics is nothing new at the Olympics. Indeed, it is often as if one follows the other around; the duo are an inseparable combination of both potential joy and strained anguish, all at once threatening to break the other down and step forward as the one thing which dominates a games. These instances can be vitriolic and shrill, such as what happened in Munich to a number of Jewish participants in 1972; they can resemble Hitler's own aforementioned spectacle of adoration and hatred doubling up in much the same way politics and sport do most summers of a four year cycle.

On other occasions, they can be subtle and allude to what is going on away from the spectacle of what you are seeing, as two people, or sides, jostle for a kind of supremacy. The rawer politic of professionalism encroaching on amateurism can arise, the likes of which hit the Olympic scene in the early 1990s, when superstar American basketball players were allowed to take part in Barcelona at around the same time the purity of the Olympic spirit was being somewhat undermined when stricter ramifications on who may and may not qualify for a Winter Olympics were introduced. These particular regulations were done so to stunt the possibility of a repeat of what we saw in Calgary, with regards to a certain British ski jumper and a certain Caribbean bobsleigh team.

In fact, there is a rich and often tragic history of the two following one another around; often leading to toxic exchanges and heightened situations where people are either hurt, scarred (emotionally or otherwise) and even killed. Looking back, what should strike the casual onlooker is as to how many of these instances pertain towards the demand for some sort of rights for a minority. What is additionally relevant is as to how politics at the Olympics begin at our very same German Olympics of 1936, the birth of the modern Olympiad, before somewhat compactly finishing at London in 2012.

Along the way, sporting contests have either turned into extensions of worldwide conflicts or continuations of domestic political stalemates wherein the athletes get a say in how their societies should be structured. Those at London in 2012 did it differently – we channelled funds to certain athletes in certain disciplines whom, physically, were what they were and were put forward to act as both the role models and success stories they were meant to be. There was no on court fighting with another nation, no rough and tumble with athletes of another disposition; there were no protests on the podium because some of them were refused certain liberties – the politic of London was different; the war had been won and all that remained was to establish to the watching world that Britain was a densely populated multi-faith island of varied races and multiple cultures.

Hitler's 1936 games were the birth of the modern Olympiad, an Olympics which was not tacked on to a world's fair or where the competitors were barely even aware that they were even partaking in something known as 'The Olympics', as was the case in the Paris Games of 1900. This was the first Olympics of the Games' official flame doing its international tour before going on to light the cauldron at the opening ceremony. This was the first Olympics to have for it an official film, courtesy of Leni Riefenstahl, whose compositions; editing styles and attempts to put together a piece ultimately did more than merely try to document what was going on.

These were the Games which ushered in the new concept of the ideal of a 'sporting triumph' going hand in hand with actual, distinctive politics. The Nazi machine had dragged Germany from the brink and was now able to boast the impressive spectacle of a packed stadium; athletes being cheered on by their home supporters and the new, invigorated flag of Germany draped proudly from its poles. Germans had a reason to feel good again about where they came from, and Hitler sought to make the world know of just how correct he was in doing what he did. Points, according to Horne & Whannel in their work *Understanding the Olympics*, were made to deliberately create the link between the mythical ancient Greek ideology of sporting and technological excellence, the likes of which saw their race and civilisation rise to the levels of supremacy that it did, and the then-modern white Nazi race, whom themselves were on the cusp of creating their own expansive empire.

Where Hitler's Berlin unquestionably began a sense of politics being synonymous with the Olympics just before the war, a very different incarnation of Berlin aided in continuing it just after in 1948. Immediately prior to the London Games' opening ceremony, an economic rift in relations between the East and West saw one half of Germany's capital begin to rot and wither away when all trade going into it was cut off. This was in sharp comparison to the West, where the controlling powers of America; Britain and France were taking care of their own respective

Berliners. This led to an event known as the Berlin Airlift, where hundreds of parcels of aid were dropped into the Eastern section of the city both over the head and beyond the desires of a certain Joseph Stalin.

The Russians were thus absent from London (the capital of one of Stalin's three main Western antithesis powers) in 1948 out of spite. It is worth pointing out, however, that they were in attendance in a scouting capacity, and took note of what was required to excel at the Olympics. By the time of the next Olympiad in 1952, the Russians were ready and finished second only to the United States whom they ran close in the overall medal stakes. It was quite the impressive debut and put paid to any doubts the Westerners had that the Soviet Union were weak, both at the negotiating table as well as in the sporting arena.

If Berlin can be viewed as the bridge between 1936 and 1948, then The Cold War can be from 1948 to 1956, and certain events once again see the Russians at the core of proceedings - this time in conflict with Hungary, whose Budapest based anti-Communistic demonstrators they took action against mere months before the beginning of the Melbourne games by physically invading them in what was an attempt to quash anti-Soviet sentiment. This spilt over into Australia's games, and in the least likely of places, thousands of miles from where it was all happening, the water polo match between Hungary and the Soviet Union descended into chaos as competitors strove to overpower one another by way of the fist.

Onwards to the issue of American Civil Rights, and the spectacle of two black American athletes who, like Cassius Clay eight years earlier in Rome, found themselves standing on the Olympic podium in Mexico City doing a nation which was yet to extend them the courtesy of allowing them to sit near the front of public transportation, proud. The now famous image depicts the respective African Americans in first and third place, split by a lone Australian, donning a singular glove each and providing the watching world with the black power salute.

The fine line of politics and sport contaminating one another at the Olympics is nary more evident when we drag such an image back to the Berlin Games, specifically as to how similar in construct both the white and black power salutes actually are. Whilst at opposing ends of a makeshift political spectrum, all that separates them is the meagre extending of one's fingers and thumb to form an indirect pointing action signifying one's admission to the supremacy of the *white* race. Merely curl them up into a fist, and you have an image not at all far from the above in craft but light years in terms of polemic.

America are again involved in the Munich example of 1972, although a little less directly. Israel's establishment as a nation state in 1948 at the end of the Second World War at the behest of the United States, and at the expense of the Palestinian people, brought about an act of violence in the already fractured German republic directed towards the Israeli athletes themselves. Garnering access to the athlete's accommodation, a Palestinian organisation known as Black September took charge of the block housing those competing in Munich whom happened to be from Israel. With chaos reigning on this, the very eve of the Games beginning, a standoff over the hostages and Black September's hold over them gave way to a bloody shootout at a nearby airport when negotiations led both the terrorist organisation and the Jewish detainees away from the initial scene of the crime.

The distinction that marks America's involvement in 1980's Olympics, taking place in Moscow, lies with the fact they had no such involvement. This came about out of the fact the Soviet Union, in all its irreligious glory, decided to invade not six months earlier one of the most devoutly religious nations in the world: Afghanistan. This angered enough Western nations to see a mass boycott by them of Moscow's Olympiad, a coalition of countries whom appeared to find allegiances in Islam during the on-going global crusade against the foulness of Communism - not because of Islam's virtues, but because it was so passionately religious where the *real* enemy of Communism was not. A similar imbalance in free, Western nations finding allegiances in places they ordinarily would not, with people they *should* not, lies quite famously, although under-documented, in the healthy relationship between America and the fascist, undemocratic ruler of Spain from 1936 to 1975 Francisco Franco – purely for the fact they were united in their hatred of Communism.

A taste of how juicy Soviet-American contests may have been at the Moscow games because of all this, on top of the initial Cold War tensions, was evident at the American *set* Lake Placid Winter Games of earlier on in the year, where a now famous ice hockey match between the two nations occurred. Within this, a team of American amateurs famously conquered the mighty Soviet professionals in a dramatic win.

In the early years of the twenty-first century, Russia *again* became an increasing worry to the liberal and increasingly globalised elite of the "free" West. For in Russia, there stood a foe who does not subscribe to the idea of a homogenised, European super-state propped up by a more globalised Wahhabi Islamic Republic in the same way the social democrats of nations such as Britain, France and Sweden do. The values and ethics characteristic of Russia at this time were reminiscent to that of what may have characterised Western Europe a hundred years earlier, at a time when Russia itself was busy casting off the shackles of monarchy and staunch religious belief before embracing a standardised republic wherein few were higher than anyone else and there was little need for elections.

By the time of the 2014 Winter Olympics, in the Russian coastal resort of Sochi, we had seen what was almost an exact reverse of either of these ideologies in each of these same respective geographical territories.

This is not to say that the West had formally abandoned their monarchies, in doing so ridding themselves of the process of voting too, but with the increasing uselessness of our Royal Families to act in the face of what we are staring down and the decreasing interest in voting for the fact little change is ever made out of our parties appearing to merge together, one must wonder just how much life either of these institutions have left. The nation of Russia was led at this time by Vladimir Putin, a man who had already openly stated as to how Russia is "...for the Russians" and denounced the European Union project – something which culminated in an explosion of activity in early 2014 when a Crimea populated by ethnic Russians was annexed into Russian control following a coup in Ukraine – the nation to which Crimea previously belonged.

Homosexuality became a temperamental issue in mid-2013 during the Moscow set World Athletics Championships, probably the most important track and field meeting in the world behind the Olympics, when Swedish athlete Emma Green-Tregaro protested (via the design on her fingernails) at Russia's recently passed laws on homosexuality, which was generally designed to discourage said practice. This legislation was accompanied by unfortunate amateur footage which arose around the time of what appeared to be homosexuals being humiliated and persecuted by other onscreen individuals, but the wider global sentiment was challenged at the athletics meeting proper when Russian pole-vaulter Yelena Isinbayeva appeared to speak warmly about what was going on before having to review her statement a few days later.

It was unfortunate that attention was once again drawn to Russia at this same time on account of their hosting of the aforementioned winter equivalent to the Summer Olympics. Sochi 2014 fell in-between both the homosexuality legislation fallout and the later conflict in neighbouring Ukraine, the likes of which embarrassingly coincided with Sochi's Paralympic Games and saw none-but-one Ukrainian paralympian partake in the opening ceremony on the grounds of protest. This was clearly an event that cut a little deeper than the situation which arose in the summer of 2008, when the South Ossetia War between Russian and Georgian forces was not enough to induce the sort of behaviour that broke out at Melbourne in the water polo pool – instead seeing a beach volleyball match involving women from both Russia and Georgia going ahead in Beijing amid hugs and handshakes.

With mere weeks to go until Sochi's opening, it appeared obvious that a political point was being made by the Russian authorities to drag the ghosts of the previous summer at the Moscow-set World Athletic Championships back into the limelight. This was put into action through the use of Russia's female curling team, whose photogenic qualities resulted in the publishing of a variety of photographs of Anna Sidorova and Ekaterina Galkina wearing lingerie. The politic was fairly evident, insomuch it seemed the Russians wanted to make it clear that *this* is what young boys and grown men should find attractive, not *other* young boys and *other* grown men. It seemed apt that the sentiment that, in Russia, we place heterosexuality *before* homosexuality, should be thrust back into the mainstream eye prior to an event as large as an Olympiad gathering. The aim was fairly distinctive, in that Russia wanted to seize on the opportunity to emphasise difference between themselves and their more liberally minded Western counterparts.

Former American political diplomat to central Asia John Herbst saw the hosting of the Olympic Games in Russia as inherently political, describing them as something Vladimir Putin could use to [8]"...burnish his own credentials as an international figure"; citing Putin's "goal" in hosting as to having a lot to do with the fact that [9]"...countries get a lot of good public relations for hosting the Olympics" and that that would also be "...true for Russia."

On the one hand, it should seem strange that this very visceral form of politics has the ability infiltrate the Winter Olympics just as easily; just as ferociously and just as, often, violently as it can the summer equivalent. We must thus reach the conclusion that there is something quite unrealistic about the calm, serene nature of everything the winter games conjures up when compared to its summer counterpart. Indeed, how could something so often inherent on the running tracks and stadium fields of a cauldron-like Olympic stadium, taking place during the heat of a summer, as people, quite literally, race one another for sporting supremacy, make its way to the colder; calmer; more sparsely populated mountains and canyons of a snowy wilderness often hundreds of miles from anywhere notable?

Almost certainly, the sense of competition is lessened, as most of the time during a winter discipline one feels as if one is competing by one's self. The contest is still *time* based, yet the competitive sensation of 'the-first-one-who-crosses-the-line-wins' inherent in the summer is lacking when compared to the winter. There is more that sensation that one is competing not against another person, but against the elements and one's own fatigue when one undertakes a cross-country skiing race; less so against a fellow shooter and more-so against the bullseye of a target dozens of feet away in a biathlon event. One is, when one ice dances, more inclined to worry about both the executing of one's routine and the prying eyes of thousands of people than what your opponent just did. When people partake in the luge or bobsleigh, they must work on their own routine and tackle the course more-so a fellow competitor, for each individual will get their own turn and that sense of one-on-one competition is more vacant.

And yet Sochi's examples are in no way the only instance of Winter Olympic events garnering political attention for means of furthering a viewpoint or ethic. Once again, we find ourselves harking back to Adolf Hitler and the Games of 1936 – this time those in the German alpine town of Garmisch-Partenkirchen, at a time when the Olympic movement staged both the summer and winter events in the same calendar year. You could be forgiven for not knowing of Garmisch-Partenkirchen's place in history as a vicious and wholly political sporting event with a specific set of ideals and designs in mind, for its place in the annuls of history is infrequently disturbed. It would of course be true to say that the Games most certainly take a seat to the side of the Berlin event of six months later, but it is still a reminder of how political these occasions can be and we must remind ourselves of the bitty, almost pathetic, ways in which Hitler attempted to instil into the people of Germany, not to mention make an advertisement to the whole world, his ideology.

In February 2014, and immediately prior to the Sochi Games, the aptly named historian Daniel Snow fronted an eponymously named documentary entitled *Dan Snow's History of the Winter Olympics*, which aired on British television. It was a programme that cut through each of the respective Winter Olympic Games to its point of broadcast and tried its best to tackle any political jousting which may have come and gone with them. The tendency to speak from a historical perspective, more-so a more raw and unabridged political one, kept the programme from being better than it might have been, but it did demonstrate how the winter sporting equivalent is culpable to being affected by a clash of ideologies or mindsets.

In exploring Hitler's Garmisch-Partenkirchen event, Snow found a Nazi policy which pertained to pushing people, whom might otherwise not be qualified for the role they would find themselves fulfilling, to the forefront of an entirely new function for what were ultimately unscrupulous means. For it was here that Hitler especially introduced the extraordinarily dangerous event of alpine skiing to the Garmisch-Partenkirchen roster, and aware of the levels of bravery; concentration and physical endurance required to tackle such a dangerous ski orientated discipline, the idea was to prove to the onlooker just how synonymous these traits were with the new, modern citizen of Nazi Germany. This meek precursor to the summer equivalent's show of Aryan strength and racial Godliness, born out of a combination of ancient Greek and Nordic physical perfection, ended up working quite well, with the gold medals in both the men and women's disciplines going to Germans.

In fact, one could remark as to how revolutionary in thinking it was that women should be allowed to engage in such a thing for sporting spectacle as far back as the 1930's. Alas, this is the fallacy that comes with utilising statistics and judging the number of women there are within a designated field more commonly associated with men as a means of success or transcendence. Was Nazi Germany a freer and more constructive society during the games of 1936 than, say, the city of Los Angeles (now a modern beacon of multi-cultural multi-racialism) was in 1932 because it had more women competing in it? Indeed, could anyone feasibly be of the opinion that Nazi Germany was superior in any way as it had pioneered the inclusion of alpine skiing *and* allowed women to compete in this dangerous-of-all skiing events where Lake Placid four years earlier had not?

No, for the means was down to Hitler's desire to prove how superior German women were to all other nations' through each of the characteristics required to conquer the alpine skiing event. This prominence, something which I hope to prove later in this work, was much in the same way that the Blairite thirst to prove to the world in 2012 that a diverse range of blacks; whites; Asians; Muslims; homosexuals, or any other minority, are more effective when conjoined together inclusively and are much more powerful when one compares it to anything that preceded their arrival in mainstream British life.

Snow also depicts one of the rare instances of Hitler actually having somebody stand up to both him and his policies, when the International Olympic Committee thought it unkind to have so many anti-Semitic signs and billboards around Garmisch-Partenkirchen during the event which informed Jews that they were "unwanted". On threat of having the Berlin games from later that year revoked should they not be removed, Hitler buckled and the Games were played out with the propagandistic signs removed. He could not, after all, risk losing the greatest global stage of all in demonstrating his political thought.

Sticking to this Jewish related tract, ice hockey player Rudi Ball was one of these Jews, yet had thus far to 1936 survived the persecution of the Nazi regime and was actually permitted to play in the Games themselves. When he did so, he did well; finding himself as a regular feature in the German team which reached the quarter finals. After the Games, he was allowed to save himself from the Nazi's stepping up of their anti-Jewish fervour, and he left Germany to settle somewhere else. Perhaps somewhat perversely, this newfound safe haven was actually the equally discriminatory apartheid South Africa, wherein he lived to his death in the 1970's.

Away from the individual examples of politics uneasily taking its place amongst the sport unfolding at an Olympics, it must not be lost that the Olympic Games have, in the past, been both used and exploited by nations looking to promote an ideology or a newfound world status. These statuses deliberately make the distinction between new and old; they are used proudly to distinguish what once constituted as the past and what now constitutes as the present. Horne & Whannel cite the aforementioned Nazi games of 1936 as an example, something which is undoubtedly true - the Third Reich did seek to pronounce to the watching world Germany's fresh ascent into the upper plateaus of first world economics and Marx-less Utopian living, minus the interference of European Jewry.

In addition to this, there is the instance of Tokyo 1964 - a games happening in a country whom nineteen years earlier (and considerably more recently than that when we realise hosts are chosen several years in advance) had two of their cities decimated by America's hydrogen bombs at the end of the Second World War. Now, half way through the 60's, they found themselves being able to host the greatest sporting show on Earth. We are reminded in Horne & Whannel again that the gentleman who lit the torch on the day of the opening ceremony was a survivor of one of those two bombs, in what was a Games designed to advertise to the world Japan's recovery from The War and onto better things.

London 2012 was another one of these instances. It was a Games which sought to establish the older realities of life in the nation, as well as its capital, before proudly exclaiming that everything had moved on and away into a freer and less stuffy incarnation of what a lot of people in the world probably thought the United Kingdom still was. A post-World War One Germany devastated by what was entrusted to be the poisonous influence of the Jew, personified in Karl Marx, was happily replaced by what Hitler had carved out of the country in 1936; Japan's association with the horrors and the evils of what they were responsible for in the Pacific theatre of World War Two, culminating in the Americans laying waste to Hiroshima and Nagasaki, was an image they substituted for this spectacle of harmony and sporting equality. The reality of the Britain which illegalised homosexuality; promoted tough Christian ethics; punished its criminals and existed in a mostly all-white, mono-cultural society was thus substituted for suave "Cool Britannia" attitudes. This was, as we shall see, and have already briefly seen, achieved through a variety of different ways.

The fact remains that whenever one pushes together, into a two week melting pot of sporting contest and national pride, different people of varying backgrounds and politics, one will often find there is some form of fallout or indifference. Modification only arrives when it is a politic that begins at the very top, as is with 1936 and 2012, and the competitors are largely allowed to compete with one another free of incident. The additional fact remains that the Olympic Games, be they summer or sometimes winter, has a precedent for acting as a host for not only sporting excellence and a fortnight of colour and exuberance, but serious political statement – whether on the track; off the track or deliberately neither.

London 2012 was no different, in spite of the fact it will feel to the majority of the British public, indeed the wider world, that it could not possibly in any way have acted in any meaningful way *as* a politically charged arena. But just because there were no abandonments; no hostage situations and no controversial statements by athletes on how they were being treated, does not mean London 2012 was not political. In many ways, London was the antithesis of Berlin. While either Games had had applied to them the exact same tactics and ideas by those at the summits of the respective projects, the overarching philosophies; policies and ideas themselves could not have been any more wildly disassociated.

THE SHARDS OF THE SPECTRUM

It is largely accepted that Tony Blair, leader of the British Labour Party from 1994 to 2007, and Prime Minister of the United Kingdom from 1997 to 2007, took his party away from its foundations without ever quite bringing them out of left wing politics altogether. For here was the Labour Prime Minister who won such large repeat majorities due to his appeal from across the spectrum; who refused to re-industrialise Britain after the Conservative decimation of these sectors in the 1980's because he largely agreed with it: the assertion that a northern English skyline dominated by factory chimneys belching out smoke belonged in the Victorian past was quite easy to get along with. Here too was someone who could associate himself with both the Democratic and Republican ideals of his American Presidential counterparts, in Bill Clinton and George W. Bush respectively, when the time came for their tenures to overlap with his own.

When, of course, the time to back America's invasion of Iraq in 2003, something being led by a brash Texan, it upset many people on the Left who were otherwise committed to Blair and his ideals, but here had them see the declaration of war an act of illegal imperialism which was cut adrift from what Labour should be synonymous with.

Blair's reinvention of the party, from being this organisation synonymous with Scargill-like characters adorning soapboxes and spouting anti-rich slogans into megaphones, to being a slick; well-dressed modern outfit for a changing neo-liberal twenty-first century is one of the great political coups of our time. Initiated by the likes of Blair, and to an extent his accomplice Alastair Campbell, this switch from grubby overalls to expensive suits; from conserving Britain's energy base and keeping the chimneys of northern England going for expensive, glassy structures such as the Shard and the Millennium Dome, should be regarded as a defining footnote in our history.

It must be said that not everyone took to Blair's New Labour ideals, with trenchant embodiment of the domestic trade unionistic left wing, and face of the 1980's miner strike, Arthur Scargill actually dismissing the bold new manoeuvre into New Labour and going away to set up *Socialist* Labour. This eventually allowed Scargill and his party to contest the 1997 United Kingdom General Election, doing so to such an extent that they were permitted a television broadcast but for their popularity in standing people. Staunch Scottish socialist Jimmy Reid, a strong speaker and once of the British Communist Party, left the New Labour set up when it became obvious things were moving away from what he always thought the left to represent. The same might be said for Tony Benn, who left parliament after Blair's first premiership in 2001 because of the disconnect he felt.

It took George Galloway, a firebrand Scot and someone deeply committed to the soul of what one might describe as actual left wing politics, until that aforementioned Iraq invasion before he fell out with those at the peak of Blair's Labour; incessantly speaking out against Iraq and consequently finding himself removed from his position as a Labour Member of Parliament. A measure as to how little things had changed by the time of March 2015 was revealed in both the actions and testament of a Labour defector to Galloway's then eleven year old party, who remarked that while it was a [10]"...huge wrench leaving Labour after more than 30 years", he had been harbouring a "...feeling for a long time now that Labour has actually left me. It's unrecognisable to the party I joined, and not in a good way. It no longer represents the aspirations and hopes of working people." Said defector went on to let off a parting shot at Labour, saying that Galloway's party now best "...represents all that old Labour was."

Many new left wing parties that appeared in the aftermath to Labour's behaviour in this regard now often run on a platform of being opposed to most of what Labour themselves stand for, in that they demonstrate allergies to the European Union; are very much against the wars in the Middle East and, in the case of an October 2005 article by Rob Ford writing for the *Weekly Worker,* are even somewhat suspicious of multiculturalism, viewing it as a Capitalist construct designed to massage the existence of the bourgeois at the expense of breaking apart the working classes. One or two of them even expressed scepticism towards the associating of oneself with things such as multi-million pound expenditures like the Olympics. Most of Blair's ideals; the politicians *like* him of his generation and the legacy of his Premierships have largely been documented in the works of Peter Hitchens and Richard Littlejohn.

We are, in fact, able to use the Olympics as a case study for as to how much Labour changed under Blair, doing so initially through Horne & Whannel's research into how a Labour councillor in Birmingham in 1993 is reported to have angrily proclaimed that they "...wouldn't spend ten pounds on the Olympics" – preferring instead, no doubt, for the money to be channelled into more constructive means such as local services and infrastructure. Thus, it is worth noting as to how the Left in this regard moved from being the sort of organisation who turn away, face clenched in abject disgust at the potential for hosting the Olympics, in to doing everything in their power to try and get it to come to their nation's capital – and all within a mere decade.

The date is somewhat important to proceedings here, with 1993 being the year immediately prior to the aforementioned Tony Blair's ascent to the leadership of the Labour Party; a position he would hold on to up to the 1997 General Election, at which point he would assume control of Britain for ten years. During this time, the party, in spite of its opaque similarities to the

Labour Party of old, in a sense continued with a Fabian legacy which began in the 1960's under *that* government – an era characterised by, aside from other things, the rise of the satire genre; the major constitutional reforms which hit the church; the civil reforms which contributed to our change in outlook on everything from our taste in clothing to sex and the beginnings of the influx of cheap sub-continental immigrant labour to fill in for work shortages.

As Prime Minister himself, Blair characterised his Premierships as being ones which would see his party increasingly find allegiance with those who believed in Islam, while they emphasised more the concept of Britain being multicultural than, arguably, any prior government. There was a large rise in immigration, the likes of which were very candidly admitted to by a New Labour speechwriter named Andrew Neather in 2009 as being a deliberate attempt to render the United Kingdom more diverse. This is very briefly explored in Kerry Bolton's work *Babel, Inc.*, wherein Neather's remarks are quite candidly revealed to have had at their core a "politically driven" social democratic desire to rock the very foundations and reshape the very makeup of British society.

With many of the top positions in various British institutions already being occupied by personnel of his generational ilk, pushing reforms through and helping to change the country into something quite radically different to the one from a generation prior was not a difficult thing, and not met with much resistance.

Winding forward to 2005, it would, in many ways, be wholly irrational for a party as viciously reformist as Blair's Labour Party was *not* to pursue the Olympic cause. For this would be a cause whereby the definition of what constituted as "patriotism" could be rebranded, as too could the very essence of what made someone 'British'. For, under Blair's watch, London became a beacon for the world, and this, twinned with the fact that Blair's Labour movement hated Britain; hated its institutions and hated what Britain always was, a diverse and multi-racial London seemed like a natural home for an Olympic Games that enabled them to showcase their core beliefs.

The Olympics, something which this country were once told they would not host but for its government's fondness for the on-going apartheid politic operating in South Africa, was suddenly something that the Left could embrace; this rather nationalistic display of flag waving, and hope that one's national side won out versus somebody else's, no longer had them feel as if they were alien to it, for what was being offered was Blair's own incarnation of Britain and its capital city: a city of blacks; Asians; Muslims and informal homosexuality, where the old guard of conservatism and empire had been all but steamrolled over for a form of socialism which was so powerful in its consensus, it was practically invincible.

In *Understanding the Olympics*, Horne & Whannel describe the International Olympic Committee extraordinarily candidly. It is a form of barefaced honesty which is near to the level of the British Broadcasting Corporation's own scathing assessment of FIFA in a 2010 documentary that aired mere days prior to the decision as to whom should host the 2020 World Cup, for which England were bidding to host: a bidding process, of which, it is believed was ruined by the BBC's work. Horne & Whannel's analysis is so scathing that one is tempted to say that had London 2012 not already been six months away from happening at the point of release of their work, it would not have had the Olympics at all.

Therein, the International Olympic Committee (abbreviated as "IOC") is described as classist; sexist and very much stuck in the past in such a way that it leads many to describe people who as are evidently bigoted. They explain its nature in the following:

> 11"The IOC was and remains an extraordinary association; not representative of nations, but with a membership that chooses its own members by the rules and within limits set by the organisation itself. The IOC remains a club based on the eighteenth century aristocratic notions of memberships with a gentlemen's club. This involves procedures such as the self-selection of members, the potential blackballing of applicants who wish to become members and clubbability (that is, members have to fit in socially)."

It is inconceivable, therefore, for us to accept that the Labour Party under Blair, and with politicians such as Ken Livingstone and Tessa Jowell all-but at the forefront of a project such as the Olympics, could associate themselves with an organisation out of similarity in characteristic or ideological agreement. In essence, these two organisations should want nothing to do with one another; the International Olympic Committee, in all their magnificence and quasi-imperialist glory, what with their criteria of selective membership; lack of openness to anyone not a millionaire and indomitable old fashioned attitude towards a range of things from women to the working classes, is the sort of organisation that should disgust a political organisation of Labour's ilk.

It was widely held that Edward Miliband, during his doomed tenure as the leader of both the Labour Party and The official Opposition to David Cameron's Coalition of 2010 to 2015, moved the party closer to its initial foundations of old-fashioned socialism and working class focus. Indeed, his election as party leader in 2010 was the trade unionist choice ahead of one or two others more inclined to be Blairite. In spite of all this, there was not any kind of desire to move the party away from the core beliefs of what the Olympics represented, and the likes of which at the epicentre of Blair's very formal cultural upheaval of the nation: inclusivity; multiculturalism and diversity propped up by a philosophy that Britain should be secular whilst paradoxically finding time to think fondly of Islam.

During said tenure, Miliband even found room to mock David Cameron during a session of Prime Minister's Questions using a more traditional left-wing right-wing philosophical dichotomy. More specifically, this lay in the fact his entire front bench were essentially millionaires; that there was a distinct the lack of women in the cabinet and that in his younger days he was a member of *The Bullingdon Club* - an additionally exclusive organisation set up for men whose own indomitable reputation for bounding through the world on a wave of reputation and influence is facilitated by chasms of affluence.

The jibe, essentially seeing Miliband attempt to establish clear difference between his party and the one predominantly in power, was made off the back of exhuming some remarks made by Cameron on how it was important his Conservative Party would bring in more female faces than were present. In what was ultimately a failure to reach this goal, Miliband jumped on the inability thus:

> 12 *"A picture tells a thousand words. Look at the all-male Front Bench ranged before us. The Prime Minister says that he wants to represent the whole country. I guess they did not let women into the Bullingdon club either.... He said that a third of his Ministers would be women; he is nowhere near meeting that target. Half the women he appointed as*

Ministers after the election have resigned or
been sacked. And in his Cabinet...there are as
many men who went to Eton or Westminster
as there are women."

In the middle of said parliament, however, was a two week spectacle brought about by the preceding Labour leaders; something that, in essence, saw a brief, grotesque and wholly hypocritical alliance with precisely this overbearing type of governing body which here instead was dedicated to international sport. Evidence, in this case, of the political dichotomy between left and right in the United Kingdom breaking down comes in the form of the fact that Cameron did bother reminding Miliband about this inconvenient truth, for he was just as in favour of everything the Olympics represented as his opposite number was: largely, the antithesis of Conservatism.

At the core of why the city of London won the right to host the games at a specially held 2005 bidding conference are two distinct contradictions, contradictions born out of fate which worked to the favour of the Left in spite of the fact the events themselves are entrenched in the almost stereotypically conservative leanings of the right. First and foremost is the item of the 2002 Commonwealth Games, hosted in England at the behest of the ruler of the Commonwealth: Queen Elizabeth the Second. This was down to the fact 2002 marked Her Royal Highness' fiftieth anniversary as the head of state, and to host the games in England (given her residence is in England) acted as a pleasant homage to that fact. What should not be lost on anyone is the fact 2012 marked her sixtieth anniversary as head of state, but that London's hosting duties to coincide with this *is* but sheer coincidence.

The 2002 Games were somewhat pivotal to London's eventual success, in that it proved to the watching world a clear demonstration that when it came to hosting these types of events, Britain was well within its capabilities. Manchester 2002 was, in a sense, the Olympic Games of 1996 it never won, and they cannot be blamed for putting on a show. So the success of Manchester 2002 was enough for those behind London's eventual 2012 bid to feel enthused that such a spectacle of sport could be put on once again – this time in the capital, and at the behest of the International Olympic Committee who would have witnessed and found confidence in Manchester. Ironic, then, how something so pivotal in inducing the ugly spectacle of falsehood that London 2012 was, was as synonymous with two things those more associated with the Left should express allergy toward: in monarchy and empire.

There exists a good old fashioned belief that the British are meant to have an allergy towards the French and everything French, in that various cultural institutions ranging from the language to the cuisine and to the writings of each nation's famous philosophers and story-tellers are alien to the other and that each side are supposed to promote their own as superior. This has been both exploited and explored alike over the centuries, in books; documentaries and films – an attitude which seems to be so embedded in the minds of each nation's respective citizens that the Renault car conglomerate produced a television advertisement towards the end of the 2000's featuring the respective cultural differences between Britain and France. The differences were exemplified in its use of either gender to 'pitch' the respective arguments for which nation is superior. How it is that two nations separated by such a tiny stretch of water can be so different to one another in a variety of facets is meant as a source for fascination and petty quarrel.

Witness the hijacking of this very traditional thought process, as documented in Mike Lee's 2006 book *The Race for the 2012 Olympics* wherein the tale of how London won the 2005 bid is documented, when the time comes to reach the passages to do with the fact the remaining two cities in the final round of the bidding were London and the French capital of Paris. Something is made of the British bid essentially conquering the French one, as if this was another 'point' in the column of the Brits during their age-old rivalry against the French within various academic; technological and sporting domains.

The sentiment from this self-proclaimed former grammar school frequenting New Labour sympathiser was a sentiment designed to induce feelings that most would tell you were antiquated and bigoted; attitudes that are throwbacks to the days of old when empire and colonial wars were the very things which made every Briton feel proud that they were as effective and as indomitable as they were. Our chief rivals, at that point in history, were of course the French, whose empire of a thousand miles away rivalled our own but whose own land was actually visible from parts of Kent on a clear day. This old-fashioned sense of patriotism that is to be invoked, due to our own ability to hold a grip over our closest rivals, is here hideously presented as a cover to the inconvenient realities of what we now actually are: without empire (indeed, even a part of somebody else's); multi-cultural and largely a Fabian society committed to continuous, strenuous reform.

Away from these two smaller instances lie several larger ones. We return to The Queen during another segment in Lee's candid book about the quest to win the rights to host something which will contribute to smashing away all that Britain once was; an instance, of which, arises when the time comes to try and spur the Olympic officials charged with voting for the 2012 host into picking London when the time comes. To try and cement the idea that Great Britain is a magnificent, grandiose and just the sort of place still wholly attuned to what it once was, in its identity; patriotism; culture and language, the powers-that-be (those in charge of the bid, of whom despise the idea of a mono-cultural , white Britain anyway) went out of their way to betray everything they stood for by providing the potential voters with a lavish dinner at Buckingham Palace full of all the stereotypical cuisine associated with the United Kingdom.

This included going so far as to serve sparking white wine from Sussex instead of Champagne, which of course is French and therefore synonymous with the opposition: the Parisian bid. These sorts of instances are, in actuality, a grotesque contradiction of philosophy when lined up against an occurrence mentioned earlier in the book when, during the Greek Games of 2004, cuisine is again at the forefront of an attempt to impress the International Olympic Committee voting base. This particular occurrence happened during an evening banquet and seminar designed to woo Olympic officials – officials who were aware that the 2012 bidding decision would be happening next summer and were intermingling with those at the forefronts of the bids. Lee recounts, with a tale set at specially rented accommodation in the dusty Greek hills, that...

> 13 *"The idea was not to serve traditional British food. This villa was not there to serve tea, cakes or roast beef and Yorkshire pudding. The last image London 2012 wanted to portray was of Britain's old colonial past. A cook brought over from Britain was asked to use local produce to prepare a melange of international specialities. The message was: 'forget that outdated image of Britain. London has changed.'"*

There is, of course, a sense of double standards here: a wish to present to the voters an idea of an England rich in culture; heritage and national identity pertaining to palaces; homemade wine and traditional cuisine, but also to stay in sync with their overall philosophy of wanting to bury much of that with the Games themselves in veering *away* from cultural items synonymous with the country. These double standards regarding the image Labour wished to *present* to the unsuspecting bureaucrat in possession of the chalice, and the reality of the very one they are wholeheartedly dedicated to prolonging, is never more evident when we observe the image of London that was presented to the world during the closing ceremony of Beijing 2008.

It begins with a strange spectacle of the Olympic "movement", here epitomised in a torch, being officially handed over to then-London mayor Boris Johnson, as the sun set on the Chinese hosting duties. This short procedure, almost a London 2012 opening ceremony miniature, actually begins with a rather wonderful choral version of both the opening and closing verses of "*God Save the Queen*" to the Union Jack being raised.

But things develop into a curious animation junket, which can only glide past red phone boxes and the old fashioned architecture, so as to feature graffiti artists; punk rockers and cosmopolitan coloured graphics of people imitating The Beatles' famous Abbey Road zebra crossing walk. Aside from the obvious Buckingham Palace, most of London's older architecture is vacant, with the Millennium Bridge; London Eye and "Gherkin" building occupying the frame – even the Spinnaker Tower, actually located in Portsmouth, finds its way into proceedings. Utilising a typical red bus roaming around the Beijing stage as a sort of centrepiece, the short stint concludes with a burst of rock and roll music hybridised with rhythm and blues before concluding with the very thing synonymous with British sport at the time in footballer David Beckham, himself just as rich in iconographic value as the buses and phone boxes, booting a football into the arena.

The point here should pertain as to how synonymous with the various aspects and characteristics of the new-age revolution of the 1960s everything seemed to be: the psychedelic graphics; the encompassing of the presence of the Beatles; the Afro-Caribbean singers, thus recognising the tremendous contribution to society black people have provided since their arrival here in the 1950's; the insistence to focus on the architectural sheen New Labour gave to London and the presence of anti-establishment punks.

So it is a safe assumption to think that no longer do you need to be of the demographic variety for whom Labour was established in order to have any kind of ties to them. Indeed, and finally on this issue, Lee speaks warmly as to how multi-millionaires Bernie Ecclestone; Keith Mills and Lord Patrick Carter poured large amounts of money into either the London 2012 project, or the New Labour movement, or both, at various points within that decade-or-so window from Blair's ascent to Labour leadership to year of Lee's book's publication. Big business; neo-liberal Capitalist economics and the vacancy of that fear of your more typical socialist government carving through the rich and compressing the class divide allows people to intermingle with Labour Party members and leaders philosophically where previously there would have been only rooted suspicion and allergy.

Strange as it might sound, and in spite of each of these aspects of the modern Labour Party we have explored, their reputation for backing large, mass marketed worldwide sporting orientated spectacles does not begin with the campaign to win the fatuous; over-egged and wholly insubstantial London Olympics of 2012. Combing back over history, there is, in fact, an instance of this that takes us to 1924. Here, at what was essentially the precursor to what would eventually become the Commonwealth Games after a series of rebranding's born out of political correctness, and unfolding at the brand new Empire Stadium in Wembley (later just "Wembley" because "Empire Stadium" too was too politically incorrect), was the 1924 Empire Exhibition.

This relatively anonymous event in an historical sense was a gathering of all the varying cultures and creeds of the empire to one place, the newly constructed Wembley venue, for a celebration over a span of about a year, all the cuisines; cultures and people living within the Commonwealth itself. After it had finished, each of the visiting empirical members would return home again and the pocket of internationalism occupying London for this stretch of time would conclude.

The exhibition as a whole was designed to promote trade as well as also remind everyone of the wonderful relationship Britain shared with her colonies. It was, as per Maurice Roche in *Mega Events and Modernity: Olympics and Expos in the Growth of Global Culture,* all about reflecting [14]"...the development of nationalism and imperialism", and was generally executed in the spirit of goodwill now often synonymous with major sporting events wherein dozens of nations come to a single place for a few weeks and put differences aside so as to compete with one another. The event was, as per the official handbook of the exhibition, and somewhat curiously by today's more modern British Labour Party standards, described by the then Prince of Wales as something which must be made to look like [15]"...a success worthy of our race."

To even both the untrained eye and the passive mind, it is a far cry from the more modern equivalent, whereby an Olympics is set in a city already submerged in a sea of foreign languages; people; cultures and differing ethnicities - each brought to it with the specific intent to change it irrevocably. The celebration has moved on from acknowledging the empire as a body of nations living in acknowledgment and feeling proud they have at least some form of fiscal trade with one another, and into a pseudo-guilt trip of self-inflicted white-hate that sees everybody *from* the empire come to London anyway.

Later Labour involvement arrives in the following decade, when evidence follows on from the above only this time in the form of the 1934 British Empire Games: the precursor to those aforementioned Commonwealth Games, whose name has undergone several politically correct shifts over time - the likes of which I already briefly alluded to. It is here that an event which, by modern standards, would be almost certainly be described as nothing less than a hideous spectacle of racism and bigotry, took place. It was overseen by a onetime Labour Prime Minister named Ramsay MacDonald, and saw a packed sports stadium witness a short window of why it was that the athletes from Britain reigned sportingly over those whom they ruled diplomatically.

If, ten years earlier, there was a sense of togetherness and longstanding-ness, best epitomised in the sheer length of the event, in Britain bringing together the best and the brightest from the Commonwealth for a meeting of grandiose fiscal and cultural magnificence, things had changed by the time of 1934. This sporting spectacle ultimately acted as a chance to celebrate empire and Britain's dominance throughout its territories, held at the empire's headquarters itself, in London, in a venue worthy of hosting such a contest – the White City Stadium, aptly named so as to technically prolongate racial supremacy in a city which was, in the 1930's, almost entirely white.

It should not come as a surprise that such a venue no longer exists, something entirely in sync with a striking observation from Horne & Whannel, who describe modern philosophy when it comes to hosting sporting 'mega-events' as thus: [16]"One of the most striking features of mega-events is how rarely they utilise the sites of previous events, almost as if they wanted to avoid taking on the ideological detritus of a former conjuncture." In this particular case, the involvement of the White City Stadium in the above example due to the fact the 1934 Games [17]"...had its origins in imperial power and racism" and consisted initially of the predominantly white colonial nations such as Canada; New Zealand and Australia. The venue, after all, was 'White' City, while its mere presence as a piece of iconography eventually came to represent all that was bigoted and outdated.

What is interesting to observe is as to how, with time passing, concepts such as these have eroded for freer and more inclusive incarnations of the Games. One could feasibly chart both the rise in counter-culture ideology and the downfall of the British Empire itself through the fact the Empire Games underwent several name changes throughout the twentieth century due to the fact Britain very gradually became less and less in possession of such a thing. The racism of these particular Games would eventually dissolve into the sort of mass-participation that saw black sprinter

Frankie Fredericks obtain a healthy Commonwealth Games record where once blacks were not even allowed to compete. In fact, conventional wisdom is as such now that it seems foolish not to think that black athletes generally will come to dominate the track events at these sorts of events; the idea that countries such as Jamaica and Trinidad and Tobago should finish outside the medal positions rendered unthinkable.

What is additionally unthinkable is the idea that, in the twenty-first century, an English team in one of these tournaments might not house at least half-a-dozen-or-so black athletes as they strive to finish top of the medal table. Where once this would have been inconceivable, it has become the norm.

Paul Jones, in his 2006 work *The Sociology of Architecture and the Politics of Building,* speaks quite revealingly of architecture and the domestic politics of the present clashing with views of generations past. Speaking of modern sporting arenas and their innuendo towards a politics of identity, in he suggests that...

> 18"...architecture may have become an
> increasingly significant expression of diverse
> collective identities in recent years. Whilst
> landmark buildings were once a central way
> of 'expressing and developing the national
> code', Jones notes that they are now
> increasingly sites of symbolic conflict and
> competition over identities. In what he
> considers to be a post-national context,
> architecture can provide a cultural space for

new identities to be expressed and contested."

We may, briefly, apply some of the above when speaking about the desire to move away from previous stadia or sporting venues for fear of association to ideology. Specifically, we may do so to the modern Wembley Stadium, which today sees a huge arch overhang it. This was a redevelopment which essentially coincided with Labour's 1997 coming to power; a project, physically initiated in 2000, which saw fit to tear down the two towers of empire that overlooked both the surroundings and field of play and replace them with a structure more suitable to encompass the modern diversity of London.

There is a deeply disturbing tale, yet eerily relevant to the London 2012 story, which involves a Brazilian slum in Rio de Janeiro named Vila Autodromo that pertains to both what the London Games epitomised and what it pertained to accomplish. It essentially begins in 1994, with a governmental realisation of an opportunity of which was presented to them on account of these same types of sporting events and the sorts of fiscal opportunities they have the immense potential to bring.

Put bluntly, the township (or favela) of Vila Autodromo was sought to be cleansed of both its inhabitants and its generally unappealing 'look' that was brought about by the reality of its low standard of citizens living there in order to make this would-be windfall a reality. Thus in their, and its, place were to be new and upmarket apartments; structures of which were to take their place alongside [19]"commercial and sports facilities" which would bring about a fresh sense of energy and a better aesthetic to the slum once upon a time founded on a thriving fishing industry, but now merely the dumping ground for sewage and society's apparent class equivalent. What might happen to the lowly citizens already occupying said stretch of fertile fiscal ground was unclear, but it generally involved something along the lines of helping them out of the way and hoping they then took their existence somewhere else.

As one might expect, the residents took against the state evicting them for sake of a boorish economic plan to do with fancy apartments and leisure facilities; eventually taking their case to remain there through every justice system in Brazil - the result, of which, was a piece of legislation which enabled them to stay there until 2034 - a forty year long stretch wherein they could at least occupy their home territory until the cycle ended and all of their woes began again.

It was unfortunate that, in late 2009, and when Rio de Janeiro won the rights to the 2016 Olympic Games, the issue of their being there returned prematurely and the forty year period of relief was prematurely halted not half way through its existence. This was down to the fact the Brazilian authorities wanted to concrete all over Vila Autodromo once again – this time with Olympic stadiums and similar sporting infrastructure.

At the core of the above is the ethic of substituting one's own for something else; something foreign, something bigger and larger in scope and scale. The ethnic Brazilians of the above are those whose homes are under threat, are being removed; relocated and, ultimately, cleansed from their own dwellings for sake of neo-liberalism and an incoming capitalist 'other'. In many ways, it mirrors London's predicament of 2012, where what was essentially a philosophy of diversity and inclusivity had forced, it was revealed by the census of a year previously, many ethnic Britons out of their London homes – the very ones wherein they had been based for generations.

Horne & Whannel present us with a brief analysis of Brazil's fiscal situation of around 2012, courtesy of the World Bank, where they point out what the wonders that hosting the Olympics will do for their country. The analysis arrives as follows:

> [20]"The World Bank predicts Brazil will go from the tenth largest economy in the world to fifth by 2016. Brazil is the fifth largest market in the world, and it has recently discovered the largest offshore petroleum deposits in the world. Funds for Olympic development come from Brazil's federal government: they would have gone elsewhere in the country if Rio had not been selected for the Olympics."

Thus, we spot the correlation between London and Rio of 2012 and 2016 when the natives to either nation are pushed to one side for sake of the potential for Capital spoil and indigenous nationalism flourishing. If there is a direct parallel between Vila Autodromo and Great Britain, specifically London in 2012, then it lies with how the governments of the respective nations treat those they consider undesirable; in other words, those upon whom vast amounts of money may be spent and those who should otherwise be favoured on account of being synonymous and indigenous to that land, in that they are thrust aside for sake of what is either sordid Fabian reformist politics or the greed of big business which lights up the eyes of those who see an opportunity to break into top-level global economics and strive to take it.

The respective natives to each of these nations stand in the way of business, much in the same way recognisable Britons do when lined up against internationalism and globalisation; the basic constructs of which are propped up by foreign investment; mass privatisation and large numbers of foreign people brought to the country from far reaching overseas places. In both instances, 'new' replaces 'old' - that is to say a fresh breed of citizen is brought in to fill in for the former occupier of a particular space. Where Vila Autodromo's is perhaps more inclined towards class in this sense, London's predicament veers more broadly towards ideas of what a racial and religious makeup might be.

One of the more astonishing admissions by Lee, in his work on how London won the right to host the Games, arrives in his frank assessment of the French Parisian bid: something which is roundly criticised as flat; monosyllabic and actually rather dull. But it is worth observing precisely what it is that Lee, present in the auditorium to witness such a thing, found so distressing about France's attempt to appeal to the delegates of the International Olympic Committee in Singapore in 2005:

> 21" ...there was a huge flaw in the overall
> presentation: it lacked real emotion – it said
> nothing about the future. On stage were the
> usual white men in dark suits. No black
> athletes, who play such an important role in
> France's sporting life, were given the
> opportunity to make a speech. Astonishingly,
> women did not play a major role in the
> presentation either."

Alas, the attempt to bring the Olympic movement to Paris just was not left wing *enough*; indeed, it just did not contain enough reformist socialism blended with a very distinct flavour of white self-loathing required to suit Lee's tastes. The idea that Paris did not win based on the above is, of course, absurd, and is if anything the barest of all admissions that London had such a distinct political hallmark behind it. As we can observe, there is evidently something about well-dressed white gentlemen that frustrated both Lee and the bidding team. Furthermore, the evident lack of blacks and women, here epitomising two of the Fabian Left's key political allies in minority ethnics and feminism, respectively, strikes him as offensive and France's punishment in this regard was to see them humiliated in the final round of voting by an outsider conquering a city who had been trying for some time to win the prize.

When the bid to win the 2012 Olympics began, the bidding team realised that they needed a manager at the very helm to run the show and ultimately be the face of the presentation when the time came in 2005 to do such a thing in front of the watching International Olympic Committee. This arrived in the hiring of a woman called Babara Casani who, in spite of possessing a track record of success in her taking of the airline "Go" from the doldrums and into a respectable name, came with one glaring flaw: she was American.

New Labour Blairite Richard Caborn commented on some furrowed brows; narrowed eyes and general murmurings upon the hiring of said woman to spearhead a British Olympic bid, evident in the following, in that he...

> 22"... likened opposition to Cassani's
> appointment to the same jingoistic criticisms
> that accompanied Swede Sven-Goran
> Eriksson's rise to become the England football
> manager. 'The nationality of the chairman is
> not an issue', Caborn told the Daily Mail.
> 'London is the most cosmopolitan of places

*and foreign leaders are now accepted in every
area of sport."*

Caborn's evident error here, at least by his own party's politically correct terms, was to refer to Cassani as a "chairman" when the more respectable term would have been "chairperson", a linguistic approach which avoids the fatal error of being gender specific in a world where any one of the two genders are able to reach the top of any given career field. When one goes out of one's ways to rewrite the rules in this sense, one should attempt vehemently to abide by them. Otherwise, genuine concerns pertaining to nationality and national pride were pushed away when they were raised about something interfering with something as potentially nationalistic as the Olympics themselves: foreign involvement at the summit of a British bid.

The immediate response of Caborn to label the questioning of Cassani's appointment as the head of London's 2012 bid as "jingoistic" is symptomatic of the attitude of the modern Left; specifically, their persistent falling back into defensive realms of having to resort to name-calling upon being posed a constructive question which might lead to genuine political discourse. Cassani was an American, an American who was initially in charge of a *British* bid to host the Olympics prior to her being replaced for unrelated reasons.

Paradoxically, London was in the running against the *American* city of New York; but the concepts of nations and nationalities, each with their own complicated set of intrinsic characteristics and dynamics, did not exist within the minds of New Labour. Thus, Cassani's appointment here essentially reduces the concept of nationhood; nationality and territories to sheer irrelevancy. For her, the appointment was just another job; it did not bother her to any moral extent that she was essentially running against her native land, much in the same way it did not bother Labour that someone not British was running Britain's attempt to host the Olympic Games for the first time in 64 years – she was merely assigned to fulfil a task.

Moving to the actual Games themselves, this irrelevance of nationhood would later translate into specific people being called upon to do a specific job within the confines of the actual stadium: evident in the aforementioned Mohamed Farah; hurdler Tiffany Porter and triple jumper Yamilé Aldama. Farah you will know of, a man whose role it was to present to the mainstream an incarnation of Islam designed to put them at ease; to break into the popular eye that Muslims are among us, living and breathing, and are British enough to run at a home Olympics and worthy of our immense support.

Aldama and Porter, you will no doubt know less of. Ms. Porter was a United States-born African-American hurdler who so happened to run under the Union Jack at the 2012 Games and the cross of Saint George two years later at the 2014 Commonwealth Games. This was after a change of allegiances, but whose role was ultimately to get more black track and field athletes out there into the wider spectrum of London's sordid spectacle and make sure that there was a stadium full of Britons getting behind a tiny piece of New Labour's anti-British politic.

The case of Aldama is so obscene that it feels almost perverted to speak of it here. Boasting the disgraceful record of having represented nations from three separate continents, this 1970's born track and field mercenary began life admirably competing for her native Cuba, before turning her attention to, of all places, Sudan just prior to winding up as a competitor for Great Britain at the 2012 Games. When the time came for her to change allegiance again (doing so for England after some murmurings it was going to be Scotland, at what would have laughably been a "home" Commonwealth Games of 2014), it effectively made her the only athlete in the history of track and field whose competing record for respective nations actually topped the requisite actions required to execute her chosen discipline. If few better epitomise Labour's borderless Britain on the track than Yamilé Aldama then few better did so off it than Cassani.

The philosophy is more broadly connected to a policy of wanting to drain the third world, or in Porter's case to take surplus from existing *first* world, of its brightest and best resources and personnel – those who might otherwise make where they come from a better place, or even proud within a sporting context. This is largely evident in the selection of the cited "British" athletes, but can extend beyond the realms of track and field to football and cricket, where home-grown players are rejected for imports in a manner that is not unlike how immigration fills in for the having to train one's own citizens up to, perhaps, become doctors or dentists. The policy, largely designed to keep the third world stagnant in its development, even forcing it to go backwards as one's own country progresses insurmountably, is far from a socialist ideal and symptomatic of Labour's detachment from their origins.

In many ways, it was one of the great hypocritical acts of Labour to select Cassani for the role, for while the New Labour movement, not to mention its successors, have persistently gone out of their way to agree to an unwritten law of equality when it comes to representatives in either their candidate selection or whatever, when, in actuality, the best person for a respective job (regardless of age; race; gender) should be what suffices, Cassani's appointment breaks that tradition.

On the surface, Cassani's appointment appeared brave and dynamic: a woman, firstly, but a foreign woman and thus keeping her deployment in perfect synchronisation with an inclusive politic. If Lee's earlier assertion that Paris' presentation was lacklustre for the fact it consisted of well-dressed white men in suits, then the hiring of Cassani should strike us as symptomatic of the politic of those behind the London bid in the first place. She was, of course, hired years before Paris gave their presentation in Singapore the night London won the bid, but we are still able to read into her appointment. That she was eventually replaced *by* a well-dressed, even privileged, white male when it appeared she was not up to task is another matter.

One of two things must almost certainly have happened in the hiring of Cassani: either that this approach blew up in the faces of those who mattered the moment she realised she could not fulfil a role she was shoehorned into, purely on the basis of being female, *or* they formally recognised her as being the best director of operations to hand when the bid was being formulated, and consequently went out of their way to hire her. Should the latter be true, Labour and those affiliated with Labour who were behind the bid essentially rejected one of their core philosophies for sake of the best in the business, thus suggesting that only the best will in fact do for Labour, but only when it is to *their* benefit.

England manager of 2001 to 2006 Sven-Goran Eriksson was alluded to in Caborn's response that Cassani was wrong for the role, and the topic itself raises some tough points; a man who was hired because he was, on the one hand, the best suited for the job at the time of his hiring, but someone who was put into a position which was still very sacred to many - one of which had never had any foreign influence in its hundred-plus year history: the England national football team and its head coach.

Criticisms of Eriksson becoming manager were directed at his nationality, for how could someone who was not English feasibly channel the passion and drive into international managing if they were not doing so for their own nation? These base criticisms hit somewhat of a reality after England's elimination from the 2002 World Cup, when squad member Gareth Southgate lamented Eriksson's inability to pump a bit of British bulldog spirit into the players at a crucial juncture of a knockout match, quipping "We needed Winston Churchill, and we got Iain Duncan-Smith."

The knives are often out anyway when speaking of the coach of England's association football team, but for Eriksson especially, it often felt as if the microscope cast a more cutting glance than usual for the simple fact he was Swedish, and if there was so much as an inkling of things not working out, his nationality and therefore his ability to really mould a group of Englishmen into a team of winners was called into question. It was as the novelty song *Sven, Sven, Sven* by an act named 'Bell and Spurling', put it: "He's a lovely geezer..." although adding "...but don't forget that he's from *Sweden*."

Statistically, Eriksson did a fine job; likewise Duncan Fletcher, a Zimbabwean who created a team of champions (at around the same time as Eriksson's footballing venture) out of whatever was left of the remnants of England's cricket team of the late 1990's. So it is possible to view two instances of two respective men knowing their sports well enough to apply their knowledge to the same field of coaching under differing circumstances: Cassani was instead involved in business and enterprising prior to the London bid, dragging certain airlines from off the chart to the heart of the industry.

What is observable here in this case study between Eriksson and Cassani, if the two even have any connection in the first place, is that in Cassani's instance, business acumen takes the place of sporting know-how - someone who likely knew about as much about Britain or London esoterically as Eriksson did, but did not have the sporting expertise for something which was, ultimately, entrenched firmly within a sporting context: the Olympic Games. Whether any of *these* criticisms are racist or jingoistic in some way is for other people to decide, but be aware that Cassani's appointment was to essentially spearhead a political project that sought to rewrite the definition of nationality anyway; thus, *her* nationality was irrelevant.

To an extent, the purity of a Briton in charge of a British Olympic bid seems about right, for who else would suit the role better than someone who could, quite literally, sell their country to a hall of neutrals deciding where to hold the greatest show on Earth? As it was, Sebastian Coe had already been appointed as the person with that responsibility when that time came to do such a thing in Singapore in 2005; but he was a man who loved the Olympics and the sporting pursuit of track and field more than anything else anyway - he fulfilled his role out of fondness for taking the Olympics to places deserved of them, regardless of the politics behind that place or the bid proper, although in this instance there was almost certainly a high probability he agreed with everything Prime Minister Blair was responsible for up to this point.

In many ways, this is the Olympic movement in its purest form as a form of conglomerate; as a business working in tow with politicians because, while they are not interested in the sports side of it, they like the idea of furthering ideology. Either way, the very fractured nature of a variety of aspects contributing to London winning the Games (the disjointed political reality of the Labour Party, the hiring of an American to front the bid, etc.) epitomise nicely the disjointed nature a city and nation was in at around this time and when the time came to demonstrate to everyone what we were.

Much of what has been discussed in this section about Labour and its core personnel is applicable to the ethic of the modern Olympics anyway, in that philosophies shift; moods change and what it is that is being presented to us, in the form of either a political party or a gold medal track and field event, has transferred into being something very different to where it began.

In *Britain and the Olympic Games: Past, Present, Legacy*, Rogan & Rogan reflect on how detached the founding sporting ideals which were imbued in all Olympic competitors is from modern day equivalents. Gone, it is asserted, are the days of amateurism occupying the core of Olympism, where sprinters would have to dig their own foot holes on the starting line; where those who might otherwise win a gold medal and have the opportunity to cement greatness thereafter had to prematurely retire for the fact they moved into coaching in order to earn the money they needed to live, and where the superstars of the day would be forced into living in a state of disgrace should they take companies up on lucrative deals to race in exhibition events away from the circuit.

The dynamic of the amateur sportsman partaking in one of these events because they have squeezed the time into their schedule away from *real* work, or studies, is all but dead at the very top of those who make their names at the Games, replaced by what you might describe as a *formula-one* style structure wherein those with the best cars that are funded by the richest people able to afford the best mechanics and technicians are the point scorers. Everyone else must consequently fall into place, wherever that may be.

There is a grim final chapter in Anton Rippon's *Hitler's Olympics: the story of the 1936 Nazi Games* detailing the life of Jesse Owens after said Olympics, when he found himself partaking in exhibition events which would see him win sprints against people whom he would give monstrous head starts and race against four legged animals under circus-like conditions so as to make money with his fantastic speed. It is a far cry from the more modern equivalents, such as Jamaican sprinter and fastest man of all time Usain Bolt, whose endorsements and advertising campaigns sees him earn a large amount of money *and* maintain the right to run.

Jessica Ennis, in her 2012 autobiography *Unbelievable*, makes an observant point about the possible correlation between track and field's lurch towards centring on success, defined by Ennis as [23]"...great financial reward", and a grander distinction between those who finish first and last and the rise in drug cheats.

In the early part of the twentieth century, a Labour Party overseeing a sporting exhibition, or having a hand in sporting arena construction, would have done so to a very different extent to that of what the Labour Party did from 2005 to 2012. Furthermore, they would have done so to events involving athletes completely detached from their respective predecessors. How this might influence people in how they view either the Summer Olympics, or the Labour Party, or both, from now on remains to be seen.

PART 2:
ATTACKING LONDON

*"THE VALUES THAT INSPIRED DE COUBERTIN WILL
COME TO LIFE OVER THE NEXT SEVENTEEN DAYS"*

JACQUE ROGGE, LONDON 2012 OLYMPIC OPENING
CEREMONY

POSTER CHILDREN

The concept of Britain possessing a quite extraordinary ability to loathe itself through the means of sporting, even specifically Olympic, platforms is not necessarily a recent trend. In spite of all of these very recent, very contemporary examples of modern stadium architecture; twenty-first century Prime Ministerial premierships and rotten bidding processes that seek to use every aspect of up-to-the-minute audio-visual modernity to get a message across, the beginnings of a discontent with society, and the way an establishment stuck in its ways runs it, goes back hundreds of years.

They lie, in fact, with a man by the name of Robert Dover, who, it may additionally surprise you to learn, is only minutely credited with sparking the re-birth of the modern Olympic movement. He did this not from whatever constituted as Greece when it happened, but instead from the humble locale of the English Cotswolds. This occurred in the seventeenth century, and was known then as the 'Olympick' Cotswold Games, staged [1]"...with some gaps for the next 250 years" and held deliberately so as... [2]"...to combat the joyless moralism of the puritans, whom he loathed".

There is little evidence that the exhibition in question was, at any point in its history, a spectacle of hate and disdain aimed solely at upsetting those to whom it was an imaginary two-fingers up, but merely a natural step in the evolution of garnering as many people as possible to the singular location of a sports track or field so as to participate in some harmless competitive sporting pursuit. The same can be said of the London games of several hundred years later, the 2012 event being almost certainly more embedded within this temperament of hatred for the past as well as those whom still existed that you might detail as "puritan" in philosophical and political thinking. The "joyless moralism" of Dover's political opponents of the day could quite easily be translated into times of more recently, particularly with regards to those that disagreed with Blair's own "Cool Britannia" revolution of ethics and philosophies – the likes of which were aggressively epitomised through the self-serving spectacle of London 2012.

By the time the London 2012 bid was being led by Sebastian Coe, a new core ideology, twinned with an all new approach to obtaining the Games, had been installed into the epicentre of it. This revolved around children, principally the motivation and desire to essentially provide the 2012 Games *for* children. Failing that, young adults, of whom might be inspired to take up a specific sport through observing someone of merely a few years older than they garnering tremendous success at the Games through participating in it. Towards the end of the bidding process, this became more and more geared towards people of *any* age, as is evident through the short film used during the bidding presentation entitled "*Inspiration*", wherein grown adults of nondescript denomination are seen to be motivated enough to partake in a variety of sports from hockey to fencing. As with so much of what the London Games would come to represent, these were represented by a broad sweep of both the class and racial spectrum.

The overarching concept that entered the bidding process pertaining to how important it was that the Games appealed to children revolved around one crucial thing: role models. Specifically, sporting personality's people below a certain age, say seventeen, could watch and feel compelled to emulate. This desire of fostering a role model in a child's life through means of sporting excellence derived from two things. Firstly, Coe's infant daughter's stark admission that such role models were all-but vacant in both her and her school-friend's lives, and that when they *were* present, they had a tendency to change in a matter of weeks.

Secondly, what meagre role models *were* present struck him as inferior compared to what they *could* be. In this instance, his children and their friends' role-models were reality television contestants, who too often amble into the spotlight without necessarily deserving to be there before quickly being replaced by somebody else. This was in stark contrast to his own childhood, where a distinct memory of an Olympic Games during a standard school day in the 1960's, where he and everyone in his class watched on as a Briton won a gold medal, told him what he wanted to do with his life and who he wanted to become.

But these points on positive role models; blunt nostalgia and the dangers inherent in looking up to reality television stars paint a layer of deception. Coe's concerns are presented as somewhat legitimate, and depending on your views on the British reality television boom of around the early 2000's, with good reason. This is until we become aware of what it is that is being presented to children as an alternative. Should you not have gathered by now, this alternative, the germs of which would have been in the organisers' minds without there necessarily being any physical manifestation of where these ideas might derive, eventually came to pass as half-caste sprinters; Muslim long distance runners and a diver who would later reveal himself to be homosexual. These would be backed up by the less physical-a manifestations propping up some of the London Olympics' less obvious political philosophies, such as the deliberate inversion of traditional gender roles and the promotion of mix raced relationships.

By the time of July 2012, the role models Coe speaks about here had unquestionably morphed into the likes of Jessica Ennis and Mohamed Farah, role models of whom would then go on to epitomise both London's post-war shift in ethnic and religious makeup and also act as the distinctive idols young people were expected to look up to as sources of inspiration.

For many years, athletics in Great Britain has been covered by the British Broadcasting Corporation, abbreviated as "BBC". Here is not the place for a more rigid dissection of said corporation, but let it be known that Robin Aitken's *Can We Trust the BBC?* deals a fairly rigid analysis of the political philosophies of its staff members going back as far as the 1980's, more specifically that they detested Margaret Thatcher, and would quite openly vote Labour, and that many documentaries and news reports throughout the 2000's were put together so as to influence the opinion of those watching. One particularly long study occupying one chapter, for instance, documents the partiality of a 2004 documentary on the Roman Catholic Church, while other more generalised content talks of a very gradual embrace of what it was Tony Blair represented once he entered the political spotlight as Labour leader.

One could quite feasibly describe the organisation now, in spite of it beginning life as a perfectly respectable broadcasting operation founded on the dichotomy of balance, as having largely gone on to become a beacon of sorts which endorses several philosophies of the modern liberal-leaning Left such as multiculturalism; diversity and political correctness. Often, their news coverage does not do the bigger picture of an event justice, as was with the case of the situation which evolved out of events in Ukraine in February 2014 or what the legacy of an overthrow of the leaders of Libya or Syria *might actually* be like.

When people who might otherwise have something dramatic or radical to say about how affairs in the United Kingdom are being run, and what the reality of certain situations are, feature on their programming, and this might include a diverse range of people such as Peter Hitchens; Nigel Farage; George Galloway; Anjem Choudary or Nick Griffin, they are treated as if a curiosity and largely outnumbered on panels or by audience members who follow philosophies more in line with the BBC's.

Indeed, when former director generals, themselves *donors* to the New Labour project, begin speaking about how the corporation is [3]"hideously white" you know you are not dealing with something that used to be what it once was. Otherwise, log on to their official website and find their news story archive, before searching for two very different names in the BBC search engine linked to being the victims of knife crime, and you will get an enormous amount of hits for the black victim of a white attack and a paltry amount for the crime bestowed upon a young man of Caucasian ilk by a gang of Asians. In this specific case, Kriss Donald, a young white man killed by Asians, returns 118 hits in 2013. At the same time, the famous case of Stephen Lawrence returns 1,448.

It is through this broadcasting organisation that athletics is generally covered via the television and radio. Up to the 2012 Games and shortly thereafter, track and field eventing was covered on a channel in the United Kingdom known as BBC Three, formally BBC Choice. There can be little argument as to the fact the channel is more broadly geared towards the younger mind, that is to say those over fifteen but probably under twenty-five. This is evident through a variety of programming more inclined to encompass bawdy humour; adult cartoons and shows which place an emphasis on one's physical appearance, although what is most important here is that this demographic possess the most *impressionable* minds of our society.

On the professional athletics circuit, something known as The Diamond League allows for runners and athletes to compete in organised events over a period of about a week at a set venue. The better they do over the course of half a dozen-or-so meetings, the higher the likelihood it is of them winning the overall event at the end of a season. It is this Diamond League to which the British Broadcasting Corporation held the broadcasting rights for all of before, during and for some time after the 2012 Olympics; a right they took up with many hours of coverage aired on BBC Three.

This allowed the pursuit of track and field to be broken into the younger, more unsuspecting minds at reasonable times of the evening during a working week during 2010 and 2011. Therefore, when the time came to exhibit such a spectacular as the London Olympics, there existed already a regimented and firm base of audience ready to absorb much more than what they have already received through the company's track and field broadcasting contract.

A concept was born out of this; an idea, of which, was so powerful in its propulsion through the propagandist basis for London 2012 that it made its way into the aforementioned London 2012 film *Inspiration* which depicted a series of grown adults living and working throughout London feeling inspired to temporarily take up an Olympic discipline within the confines of their own profession. So, for example, a street cleaner begins to use his broom as a hockey stick; some trash as a makeshift ball and two skips as goal posts.

A second short film, used during the Singapore presentation, depicted poor African children sitting beside a makeshift road running through a desolate village who are wasting their time tossing stones at a steel can. With commotion radiating from a café behind him, one of the boys turns and is just in time to see the final of the London 2012 one-hundred meter event. There is a sense of it inspiring the child into sporting action. This film in many ways epitomised Coe's new politic he brought to the project, one which was all about doing something to *create* figures of inspiration; to *create* athletes who had the potential to stimulate children and teenagers to take up sport.

So the utilisation of characters such as Ennis and Farah, as folk embodying the various ethnicities; faiths and so forth slowly being broken into the minds of the watching youngsters, thus promoted the idea that not only should attitudes and creeds such as Islam and the engaging in mixed-race relationships be removed from a status once associated with being devious or alien, but should actually be reintroduced as acceptable and apart of the mainstream – and all delivered under the guise of inspiring people to take up sport.

In many ways, diver Tom Daley, upon revealing himself to be homosexual in December 2013, only really became a part of this cycle later on – a photograph he took of himself during a diving tournament in Russia in 2015, with the Kremlin placed deliberately in the background, was a statement on that nation's attitudes towards homosexuals and cemented the point. Boxer Nicola Adams too, as the Games got closer and the British Olympic rosters were being filled, found a way into this cycle as a female who happened to box. The dramatic achievement of the male gymnastics team, who won a medal against all historical and statistical odds after a sudden disqualification above them, only really seemed to become an aspect of this as well when the moment came for the announcer to inform the audience that Britain had indeed won bronze.

The relevance of Adams here is made more apparent when we observe the point made by Horne & Whannel which pertains to how the broadcasting of Olympic disciplines during the Games themselves which involve women more often than not focus on events that accentuate figure or good looks. This is found, for instance, in the likes of diving; beach volleyball and swimming. Whilst it is mentioned, we will waive the pursuit of track and field for the fact such a thing is the essence of the Olympics anyway. Thus, too often under a veil of equality and the idea of women receiving a balanced representation during a broadcaster's airing of the Games lies a seedier truth:

they are allowed airtime, as long as they look whilst it's happening.

Using the idea of how the London Games of 2012 were a means to showboat Britain's New Labour fuelled inclusivity, and pertaining directly to the depiction of female boxers and the male gymnasts, we see attempts to invert a norm which breached new ground in its bothering to depict women at all, albeit via some rather hypocritical means, but are now desperate attempts at revisionism. The results could not have fallen in Great Britain's favour any more than they did, with Nicola Adams winning what was the inaugural boxing tournament for women and the male gymnasts worming their way into a bronze medal position after a disqualification above them – their first medal of any colour in the event for several decades.

What is vital at this point is to establish that what unfolds at an Olympic Games has the very real and very powerful ability to influence upon the hosting nation the kind of society a politician might want to build. One of the more famous instances of this, that is to say: large sporting events being used to mould international opinion on a location or domestic opinion on an ideology, occurred in 1995 when the Rugby World Cup in South Africa was more broadly used as a means to unify a country, or 'sell' a political ideology of socialism and equality, through sport.

It is often the case also that an Olympics, or similarly sized event, will arrive with promises of a legacy. This is often one of economic stature, but it may stretch to encompass the less beneficial sounding of allowing a nation use of stadia capable of facilitating future sporting events or music concerts. The stadium used during the 2002 Commonwealth Games was, for instance, utilised by English football club Manchester City as their new home ground. Most home games contested by the national football team of Greece are done so in the Olympic Stadium of 2004, while Wembley itself has acted as the neutral venue to numerous footballing matches across several competitions. More recently, it has been used for charity rock concerts and overseas American Football League (NFL) games.

Various ideas and proposals have come and gone since the end of the London 2012 Games with regards to its own respective stadium. These have ranged from the potential it might have in hosting a twenty overs aside cricket match involving Essex County Cricket Club to numerous wrangling's involving West Ham United football club making it its permanent home stadium. Views on other aspects of the 2012 Games' legacy, however, arrive in different shapes and sizes. In the opinion of Rogan & Rogan, for instance, the true test of the London Olympics' legacy will lie in as to whether or not obesity levels have dropped to a certain point. They additionally remark as to how it ought to have had some sort of positive bearing on the fiscal situation the country found itself in as a consequence of the 2008 financial crisis.

Ultimately, one can only really entrust the legacy of the London Games to be that, through a variety of personnel propelled into the spotlight because of it, the [4]mixed-race marriage will be more common; conversion rates to Islam will increase; traditional gender roles will become increasingly inverted due to the impressive achievements of Nicola Adams and Max Whitlock, and the acceptance of homosexuality so prevalent that should you be in your twenties and yet to have had a homosexual experience, you will likely be looked upon as being in opposition to the mainstream.

The idea is backed up by the aforementioned Rogan & Rogan, who, away from their taut theories about obesity and economics, look at 'on field' legacy and what it means to have been a part of the success of it:

> 5 "The great irony, of course, is that despite all of these grand legacy plans which relate to the Games, history tells us that they do not define an Olympic Games in the memory of the population at large. That is the job of the home nation team. Australians recall Cathy Freeman's victory in the 400m as providing a national sentiment which continues to run far deeper than resentment at the white elephant of an Olympic Stadium in which she won that gold medal. Canadians in the aftermath of the (2010 winter) Vancouver Games already find it hard to look beyond

> *their victorious ice hockey team who beat the*
> *United States in the finale event."*

Indeed, the on field legacy as opinionated by these writers appears to be the one item capable of making more of an impression than anything else. Fans, particularly the younger ones who were targeted especially, the likes of which we have already explored, will take away from the Games a message built on foundations of diversity and inclusivity: that pluralistic societies consisting of black people; white people; mixed race individuals; Muslims and homosexuals all being allowed to occupy the same space and being allowed to compete under a flag that has been contorted to represent the essence of multiculturalism, is normal. This demographic of people, too young to think or necessarily form opinions on anything, fear not for economic strains and nor do they worry while the Games are on as to what happens to the stadium the week; the month; the year after the event has finished.

If the legacy of the London Games is to undertake any resemblance to the above example involving Freeman, then it will almost certainly epitomise the true essence of multiracial, multicultural socialist Britain: we may very well be poorer economically for whatever reason, but we at least possess one another: the differing creeds, cultures and racial diversity, and *that* will be what keeps us going...

A CLASS APART

Pierre de Coubertin was a Frenchman born in the nineteenth Century. Like his compatriots Jules Rimet and Henri Delaunay, with regards to the FIFA World Cup and UEFA European Championships respectively, he was largely responsible for the reigniting of the Olympic movement that has evolved into what we know today. De Coubertin himself lived a fraught, eventful life; one which began in 1860's Paris, encompassed a Catholic upbringing, a son who died aged two and financial troubles that were so crippling that he lost close to everything. In spite of all this, he was married (to a woman who lived long enough to see the first half of the twentieth century, dying aged 102); was a well traversed man, who took particular interest in Great Britain, and extremely well read. He died in 1937, at the age of 74.

The whole Olympic ethos is, in some sense, built on the life narrative, not to mention attitudes; characteristics and visions, of this one man. Part of the reason, as has been established, that Britain made for such a good host in 1948 (and then later in 2012), but would have made for a lousy one when they bid in the 1980s, is linked directly to the personal ethic of de Coubertin and his life experiences. More specifically, this lay in the fact Londoners were able to display a startling amount of solidarity in being able to repel the

Nazi menace, while forty-nine years later Blair's own rebranding of Britain as a global hub for the world's best (and worst) to come and enjoy life stood in stark comparison to Margaret Thatcher's own domestic policies, twinned with her sympathy for South African Apartheid rule, of which we will come to, and of which ruined Britain's chances of hosting the Games.

Principally, de Coubertin was a socialist on top of a variety of other things. The man's general ethic is summarised in the following:

> 6 "He (Coubertin) was influenced by socialist
> theorist Frederic LePlay who, concerned at
> the impact of class division, sought means to
> restore peace and harmony. He believed that
> sporting competition between all the nations
> of the world could lead to mutual
> understanding and respect between
> individuals of different nations, races and
> social positions."

One very specific and very delicate event that influenced his thinking and desire for what would become the Olympic movement was the fallout from the Battle of Sedan, fought during the Franco–Prussian War of the nineteenth Century. Horne & Whannel describe the national mood in France at this time as being full of shame, complicated by the 1870 Republication of the country and the later ceding of territories Lorraine and Alsace to Germany, a neighbour of whom it was rightly considered were rising to be more powerful. It would appear that these events, unfolding in a sort of perfect, sordid synchronisation, frightened de Coubertin in that he was influenced because of this to try and provide the world with a sense of unity where so much of his youth within his immediate geographical locale at this early age was full of discontent.

It is important here to both recognise, as well as dismiss, accusations of nationalism in de Coubertin's actions later on in life. To label him nationalistic would be wrong, for de Coubertin should strike us actually rather allergic to nationalism – the likes of which propelled the events that shook his childhood. That the Olympics have *become* more nationalistic as time has elapsed, or even become more associated with *nation* in the sense of politicians wanting to use the Games to highlight ideology, is not to say that they began as they exist now.

This is evident in the fact that it was France, and Napoleon III in particular, who declared war (an inherently nationalistic action at the time of its happening) on the state of Prussia which led to the Battle of Sedan in the first place, while the collapse of the Second French Empire in 1870 suggests that in order to avoid national humiliation in crumbling to defeat in the colonial stakes, avoid the notion of colonialism in the first place.

Furthermore, the ceding of the aforementioned Lorraine and Alsace territories to neighbouring Germany is an instance of one nation growing larger

off the back of another's national shame, events of
which led to one territory growing stronger and the
other weaker when the desire ought to be to unite and
live in a state of harmony. It is worth pointing out at
this point that Adolf Hitler would later refer to French
forces invading and occupying German territory around
this area as Germany's *own* national shame, thus
cementing the link between the fates of nations; their
empires, in the form of territory they may or may not
own, and nationalism.

It would be apt too to here point out as to how,
what is now referred to as the European Union, has its
origins in this same geographical location in that one of
its core founding goals was to unite the French and
Germans not long after the above in the aftermath of
World War One. This was, you understand, an attempt
to reconcile either nation's differences in a compromise
whereby they could share these generally coal rich
territories. That many of the mainstream parties in
Great Britain at the time of the Olympic Games stood
on platforms of wholehearted Europeanist attitudes
should come as no surprise within the greater context of
this work.

In the case of Hitler, we of course witness the very
dangerous consequences of where this line of thinking
can lead. The second point on this issue of de Coubertin
growing up and wanting to undertake a politic of unity,
more-so than division, is more broadly related to class –
specifically, the gap in class with reference to sport and
those who are more traditionally associated with the

playing of certain sports over others. The latter half of the nineteenth century was a very important time for global sport as a whole, with the 1896 Olympics being this instance of the whole world (or very nearly the whole world) becoming unified for the item of sport – this would continue on into the early part of (and indeed conclude in) the following century whereby the establishment of the football World Cup in 1930 would occur.

International sport, that is to say contests between personnel from two specific countries, was becoming more prominent at around this time: golfers were traversing the Atlantic to do battle in respective U.S. and British Opens; cricketing tours saw England travel to Australia (and then Australia back to England) to contest what would quickly become "The Ashes", and the first international football match ever contested was England vs. Scotland, with England later frequenting continental Europe to battle places such as Bohemia and the Austro-Hungarian kingdom. But the people partaking in these sporting contests were always specified by their class variant, so rugby and cricket were exported to the nations of the British Commonwealth but football (a working class game) found only a home in South America. Hence, we witness cricketing powerhouses in the form of countries like India and New Zealand standing in stark difference to the footballing reputations of somewhere like Argentina.

To cement the point, I must call upon an article by John Carlin which speaks about the birth of football *in* aforementioned Argentina; an article published in a 2002 paperback almanac previewing that year's football World Cup. More specifically, the piece recounts the British involvement in popularising the game in Argentina at the end of the nineteenth century; explores the roots of the domestic Argentinian footballing set up and observes that a number of modern Argentinian football teams bear English names for the fact English engineers and labourers took it with them to the country when deployed at around this time. Carlin reminds us that...

> 7 *"It was an English schoolteacher who founded the game in Argentina. Watson Hutton came to Buenos Aries to be headmaster of Saint Andrew's School. But he is remembered for starting the first Argentine football league in 1891. Not that local players were allowed a kick in those days. All five teams in that first league...were made up of British players."*

He goes on to establish that in...

> 8 *"...no other country where Spanish is spoken does the original English terminology, or something very much like it, permeate the language more than it does in Argentina. In Spain, Spanish words are used to describe a*

corner, a centre forward, a winger. In Argentina, they still say 'corner', or 'centro-forward' or 'wing'. Nor has it occurred to anybody to change the utterly English names of so many leading English clubs – River Plate, Racing or Newell's Old Boys."

These ideas are not necessarily synchronised with that of what Horne & Whannel have offered us, in that Carlin asserts that the first league championship of Argentina did not even allow for native Argentinians to take part due to thoroughly British squads of people engaging in the game – thus having it sound like just another extension of imperialist British rule. It is asserted by Horne & Whannel that *working* men took the game to South America, but the scenario of manual labourers taking the game somewhere new; recognising the hardships of their new surroundings as they did back home and inviting the newfound people to join in seems lacking in Carlin's story, where a stuffy teacher, who sounds as if he was as much a part of the imperialist establishment as anyone else, made up the rules of inclusion as he went along. In spite of this, it is the *ethic* of the historical footnote that is generally the same; certain prejudices and distinct ruptures in class divides were apparent in the exporting, registering and then playing of specific sports in specific places, and it was this which de Coubertin strove to eliminate.

de Coubertin was well aware of these numerous divisions by the time he reached adulthood, and thus undoubtedly felt inspired to bring about what would eventually become the Olympics' core ethic of "Olympism"; something driven by the accepting of those different to you, no matter how divided on the class scale, and accepting that it would be better if divisions and differences were laid to rest. London 2012's skewering of this ideology was to encompass a fresh new era, one of coexistence with other people where previously there could only ever be malice and new, enhanced acceptances that everything in force for so long should be scrapped to make way for an age free of right wing conservatism.

de Coubertin's vision held steady for the first few editions of the Olympics, with sports that carry a more opulent bourgeois reputation such as golf and tennis co-existing with the as-established working man's game of football – all three of which were lumped in with the usual track and field disciplines which went right the way back to the era of ancient Greece. This waned as the years progressed, with various disciplines coming and going, but Britain's determination to spike de Coubertin's ground-breaking ethic in 2012 with the aforementioned racial; gender; class and faith based gentrification kept the remnants of what the man started a century ago ticking over to a basic extent.

We witness this hosting of the Games in 2012 as an unquestionable continuation of the aforementioned ethic of how "sporting competition between all the nations of the world could lead to mutual understanding and respect between individuals of different nations, races and social positions". Specifically, how separate nationalities; ethnicities and cultures already based *within* Great Britain (or London specifically) could be united through the means of sport which would *further-still* allude to a larger political unity that was desired by the people who brought the Games to the country in the first place.

One instance of both racial and class identity being shredded as a consequence of the 2012 Olympics arrived during a New Year's Eve 2012 airing of a documentary entitled *Olympics 2012: 50 Greatest Moments*. This self-explanatory programme was aired by that indelible British Broadcasting Corporation (and on BBC Three, no less) and ranked the best moments from that summer's Games. One such contribution came from a black gentleman who made a living as a rap musician, who, when asked about his memories of Charlotte Dujardin's gold medal in the individual dressage event, recounted an amusing story involving him; a group of other black youths, with whom he was having lunch that day, and the fact he openly exclaimed his frustration in front of everyone the moment he suddenly realised that he had forgotten to set up a machine at home to record the final because he knew he would be out.

This was due to the fact the spectacle of individual dressage, an otherwise elitist sporting practise engaged in by a privileged class, had made such an impression on him during the Olympics that he was looking forward to the gold medal event. Finding himself away from a television on the day of the final, however, he suddenly realised that he had no way of even watching it later on at his leisure. Within the discussion, he took time to mention his accomplices' reaction to his very public frustration, which needless to say was of immense surprise at a newfound interest in something which should, otherwise, seem distant and obscure to him.

Thus, we witness the power of the Olympic model as something which draws people in to circles and realms otherwise disconnected from them. This individual instant was likely all but a mere snapshot of what was unfolding within the wider realms of the United Kingdom during this sporting fortnight, as many millions of people had their minds and eyes opened up to, not only new sporting disciplines, but philosophies and ways of life.

Indeed, the British Olympic team as a whole very much consisted of this mix of blacks; whites; Asians; homosexuals; Muslims; millionaires; amateurs; professionals and people with connections to the royal family. One or two competitors may even have been a combination of two or more of the above. This was the Olympiad whereby the Somali born Muslim Mohamed Farah could walk out alongside homosexual Tom Daley, furthermore alongside an array of Anglo-Caribbean runners. People of whom you had never heard, such as handball player Robert White and women's water polo squad member Frances Leighton, could take their place beside household millionaire sportspersons such as Andrew Murray and Ryan Giggs.

From Rio de Janeiro in 2016, fabulously wealthy golfers such as Tiger Woods and Rory McIlroy will too be able to take part.

London 2012 essentially saw a raw, unabridged version of what de Coubertin sought would become his legacy for decades; his views and opinions finally finding a resting place in one of the world's multicultural capitals in an era of big business-driven neo-liberal internationalist globalisation, something propped up by mass-immigration and a fondness for the private sector, where some, or most, of London's actual modern landmarks are owned by foreign people thousands of miles away.

In one sense, de Coubertin's vision to unite nations and induce a peaceful procession of sport was hijacked by the mainstream Fabian Left for their own means, for de Coubertin ultimately remained an advocate of nationhood and the idea of a person being able to call where they lived their home. As the decades went by after the man's death, and Olympic meetings came and went, we witnessed, at the best of times during occasions of strife, boycotts that saw entire nations staying away due to disagreements on political grounds. At the worst of times, we saw fights breaking out between athletes during water polo matches and more humbling incidences such as the massacre in Munich. It would of course be foolish to say that the Olympic Games has been responsible for making the world a worse place, indeed even contribute to a downfall in international relations, but it is remarkable as to how often it has been used by people as a worldwide stage to *create* political protest, often to extreme extents.

THE ATHLETE'S GLOBAL VILLAGE

In their book *Understanding the Olympics*, Horne & Whannel cite a 1984 work by Jim Riordan entitled *The Workers' Olympics* and briefly describe how a separatist Olympic movement was set up in the 1920's to spite what was seen as an unpleasant, inherently bourgeoisie exhibition of competition whereby the winners were too distinct from the losers and where the concept of people competing for countries was too prominent. Principally, these rebel Olympics, set up in opposition to whatever constituted as the Olympics in the aftermath of World War One, were designed more-so to promote the philosophies of 'internationalism', seen here as the antitheses to the 'nationalism' the existing Games offered.

In addition to this was the adverse reaction to the Olympic movement's elitist encouraging of only the best and the brightest to take part, something which would eventually whittle the field down to a handful of competitors, wherein a winner would emerge from a group of top athletes who only came from a mere two or three nations. In its place, the concept of "mass participation" – essentially two fingers up at the approach of worming out the best of the best from a select few. Thirdly, and in spite of Baron de

Coubertin's attempt at amalgamating sporting pursuit with socialist philosophies, the Olympics at the time were largely seen to be exclusive to the rich and privileged; a movement overseen by a benevolent and discriminatory governing body that did not like [9]women competing and appeared to restrict participation to the young, affluent sons of the rich. In its place, the organisers, who had strong connections to the internationalist worker's movement, sought to try and encompass the opposite.

Lastly, this same organisation movement did not believe that the goal of true amateurism, not to mention this authentic sense of people 'coming together', could be achieved through differing flags and anthems which did nothing but differentiate people from one another. Instead, the opening ceremonies did away with such things and athletes stood around singing Leftist hymns such as *The Internationale*. The last of these Workers Olympiads took place in Antwerp, in 1937; an event which had to be rescheduled to that time and that place on account of the outbreak of the Spanish Civil War interrupting the planned Barcelona meet in the previous year. This was, by chance, a war which happened to involve most of those who had turned up to compete in these Workers Games anyway, and thus instead of spending their time in Spain running, jumping and throwing within a sporting context, they instead took up arms for the Leftist charge against Francisco Franco.

In many ways, there exist a range of connections between this very Leftist; highly revisionist and extraordinarily Fabian version of the Games from decades ago, and what we witnessed in London in 2012. First and foremost, observe the tendency the modern British Labour movement, the organisation responsible for the 2012 Games, have in closing their annual conferences with a singing in unison of a variety of hymns synonymous with the revolutionary Left.

Abolishing flags; anthems and nationalities for London 2012 was of course wildly beyond the Labour Party's control. Instead, the makeup of the British team was tampered with in such a way that black people; white people; Muslims; Christians and even descendants to the British throne were suddenly summoned together under one banner in an immense statement of unity which came to constitute as the encapsulation of what the Worker Games of yester-year were all about.

Additionally, and prior to the medal ceremonies during the London Olympics themselves, Vangelis' theme from an immensely popular 1981 film entitled *Chariots of Fire* was played; the music came to represent a sort of anthem within itself, and essentially acted as the main piece of "Internationale-esque" music which would enjoin all athletes who were about to receive their medals before the *actual* national anthems would play. Pertaining to the idea that "mass participation" is more important than the brightest and the best almost exclusively being allowed to take part in the Olympic disciplines is the situation which arose when the time came to select those who would be

representing Britain at taekwondo. Put simply, white
Briton Aaron Cook was pushed aside for the more
inclusively sounding Lutalo Muhammad; this is in spite
of the fact Cook was both a reigning continental
champion in his class and the world number one at the
time of the selections.

Vitally, we must observe that Muhammad was no
slouch in the respective discipline - he went on to win
bronze at the London Games, but the situation quite
clearly has its origins in this more contemporary
approach of attention-to-diversity-thru-selection
blended with a much older, more traditionally Leftist
approach where one shuns the skilled and informed for
the sake of bringing everybody into the game. The
excuses and exclamations for the reason behind this
should fall on deaf ears, for ultimately it must be
realised that this was a situation whereby the name
"Muhammad" was seen to look better on the team sheet
than the more traditionalist "Cook", purely for the fact
the former epitomised more this newfound era of
diversity.

In many ways, it mirrored the scenario at the Berlin
Games of 1936, detailed in Hilton's *Hitler's Olympics:
The 1936 Berlin Olympic Games*, where German high
jumper Gretel Bergmann was this time *excluded* from
the team for no apparent reason, in spite of the fact she
was demonstrably the best high jumper of German
nationality. Ultimately, we are able to look back on the
fact she was Jewish in order to deduce why.

On the 2012 London Olympic site in Stratford City sits a structure named the Westfield Mall. This was in its own right a vital component to the Olympic experience; a large, post-modern building which was erected to quench each of the frequenters of the Olympic Games' shopping and materialistic thirsts. Occupying a page in Horne & Whannel's *Understanding the Olympics* sits a photograph of this shopping precinct under construction at some time in the late 2000's – amongst the mud; machinery and workmen sits a billboard proudly sporting the phrase "Welcome to the Next Generation".

This is significant for two reasons, the first of which is that, put simply, the structure itself was built on the site of where the entrance to the *old* stadium which hosted the 1908 Games used to be. As discussed, this particular exhibition was a Games from a bygone era, an era of racism and imperialism; an era that has been instilled into the minds of the modern Briton as one full of bully-boy tactics overseas, as we behaved disgracefully; extended our empire and took without giving. The whole purpose of the 1908 edition, as well as the Empire Games (later the Commonwealth Games) that followed, was to instil into the watching audiences Britain's supremacy over the rest of the world - first through their wonderful ability to trade, and then later through their physical performances in vanquishing the inferior minions of the commonwealth. As discussed, the overhaul of the old Wembley Stadium and its two awkwardly placed imperialistic towers stands in sharp contrast with the new post-2007 arch, which has its roots in this post-New Labour era of unity through reform.

The relevance of the billboard and what it says is obvious, in that the "next generation" is very much New Labour's proposed ethnic and cultural shakeup designed to eradicate everything the United Kingdom was for hundreds of years; perpetrated and exemplified in the Olympics themselves while epitomised in the readout from the large sign. The 'generation' in question is, of course, the generation of multiculturalism; the generation of the mixed race marriage, the all but complete abolition of sovereignty and the blurring of one's national identity with a combination of European Union membership and mass immigration, not from forward thinking places with millions of decent, well-mannered citizens such as New Zealand or South Korea, but the third world and all the hideous things that come with that.

The "next generation" is each of these things paving over the things which defined the old generation, that of identifiable sovereignty; old fashioned systems of education; liberty away from prying governmental acts; monoculturalism and properly enforced law and order. The paving over of the sites which represented all of this, or belonged to eras with much of the opposite of these things in force, with something very new and very different is evident: this is how civilisations replace one another.

The second reason that the construction of the mall is significant lies with the subject of trade, with the point well summarised via a short, sharp snide at the comparison between old and new thus: [10] "If in 1908 the focus was on trade and production, by 2012 the focus is very much spectacle and consumption – courtesy of the shopping mall." True, for where the Olympic meetings once had their roots in world fairs and trade exhibitions, and that the likes of London could boast such a thing in 1908, a century later things were very different. Where once we produced, we are now largely de-industrialised and enjoy consuming the produce that arrives from foreign countries such as China and America – some, if not most, of which we do not even require or could indeed produce ourselves, more competently, should we feel like we needed it.

If 1908 and, to varyingly similar extents, 1925 were thus too imbued with the triumphs and wonders of colonialism and the celebrating being an entirely white nation, so too were they too synonymous with anti-globalist sentiments more broadly linked to trade and domestic production, where one might coin one's own innovative creations and inventions before taking them along to a world fair with the distinct intent on exhibiting them and furthering one's own supremacy in the global innovative stakes.

2012, then, was something else. It was, put bluntly, a celebration of our newfound ability to consume. It was a celebration of how de-anglicised Britain had become, a perverse championing of everything that had happened post-war in the immigration stakes and then furthered by Blair's newly reformed Labour Party who sought to retain most of the Thatcherite economic approaches whilst systematically undermine a nation that was always seen as this indomitable, backward and wholly intolerant place living off a sense of empire and self-congratulation.

With regards to class division, there remains a tremendous amount of spite at the very peak of British politics; sentiment, of which, is more than apparent in *Understanding the Olympics*. It is asserted, through research into those who took part and won medals, that too many of the athletes representing Great Britain in the 2000 and 2008 Games came from privileged backgrounds – epitomised in where they had their educations, namely at private and independent schools. It was largely accepted as unacceptable that so many of Britain's medal winners, predominantly in events such as rowing and sailing, would be of such a distinguished ilk and would be representing many millions of people who had not had, nor were currently living in, the rarefied stratospheres of such backgrounds as these people were. Put simply, the concept of a council flat dwelling tenant cheering on a rich and privileged oarsman was unfathomable.

There is almost certainly something wrong with being a gifted child in the post-Blairite Great Britain; children, regardless of ability, are made to suffer in comprehensive schools with batches of other children from varying backgrounds and abilities rather than proceed forward with others of their distinguished ilk in evidently better places of learning. The rich and the privileged are looked upon with scorn by the very people who have moved into the exclusive Westminster circles so as to become precisely this. They are forced into adhering to the anti-British policies of a Fabian elite who preach the very things we saw in abundance during that sham of a two week period in the summer of 2012; ordered, even, to accept a new breed of diversity and equality when came the waves of experimental mass immigration designed to displace the white population.

The ultimate goal is to unite, through inherently classist policy, the people of Britain into one large multi-racial multicultural state wherein each are encouraged to subscribe to their own ways of life whilst maintaining a sense of pauperism and grounded socialism whereby no one class or ethnic group may exceed the other. This gentrification goes a long way in eradicating the above discrepancies and discriminations, where the idea that damage was being done got into the heads of those actually implementing this damage should they not press on with their policies of inclusivity.

What might be the beginnings of this in a more recent time, away from Mr Dover's aforementioned Cotswold Games designed to spite people of a purer and more moral sort, lies in an example from Rogan & Rogan. Here, esteemed British rowing club Henley saw an unfortunate incident sometime in the early twentieth

Century wherein the established elite were upset by a ragged group of foreign newcomers; a group of people whose rowing ability embarrassed those who were expected to win easily in a race:

> *11 "When Henley's restrictions were breached by a Canadian crew which won its race easily, further rules were imposed to prevent 'artisans, labourers or mechanics' competing. The impact of this decision was to reduce the potential talent pool for British rowing considerably, which damaged its international standing in the sport for decades."*

The Canadians, it would seem present in the race illegally, put the idea of class usurping talent to the sword with a fantastic display which even in the early years of the twenty-first Century, is finding its way into books on the Olympic Games. In the aftermath of this, the decision to go in a very specific direction – to discriminate even further against those from entering, thus conserving Henley's classist purity in the calibre of people who may row there and compete there, is interesting when lined up against more contemporary attitudes of inclusivity. My attention is drawn to the idea that the deciding on this course of action diminished the rowing talent pool in Britain even more, where had those of the Canadian's lowly class type been permitted to further compete at rowing, it would have grown. Because it did not, our standing in the sport was seemingly damaged for decades.

Political philosophies in place for London 2012 were specifically designed to make it so that instances such as this would never befall Britain again; would never see such discrimination whereby there was, or might otherwise have been, an interest in a sporting discipline which would usually only be synonymous with a definitive 'type' of person. Britain's place on the international stage with regards to its Olympic stature, the likes of which you might say peaked in a statistical sense at London 2012, has been made noteworthy again through precisely the use of the above ethic.

This was through a very specific application of a very specific set of sporting personnel to the British team as a whole, a set of personnel that included the likes of the stalwarts Ennis and Farah, whom we should know by now, but also the implementation of citizens of the former empirical colonies where previously there were none, in order to improve our standing in the world of sports. Thus, we are able to witness a marriage of the above philosophies with the Left's policy to generally implement the citizens of the world *upon* Great Britain through the means of mass immigration designed to improve our standing on the world through a neo-liberal economic model.

Just briefly, one particular similarity between Hitler's 1936 Berlin Games and the London Games of 2012 lies within the issue of professionalism within athletics. With Hitler in charge and administering Nazi policy to the German economy, the country made a rapid ascent from being what it was into being the sort of superpower capable of doing what it is that Hitler is broadly more famous for doing. This enabled the German athletes at the time of the Berlin Games to be state sponsored, something which would all-but-guarantee their victories over a field of other athletes, of whom were still making their own way in life and funding their own programmes through work away from track and field practice.

This is not unlike the modern day equivalent, where a number of Western nations, no less Britain, do not, on occasion, put their respective athletes through the worry of where funding is going to come from. Indeed, within the modern British Olympic setup, and with this state driven reality in mind, the lynchpins of those funded such as Ennis and Farah effectively become political pawns - people recruited and manipulated into these wonderful athletes whose personal goal it may be to win Olympic gold, but whose longer term purpose is to assert, like the Nazis, the supremacy of a political ideology when the time for the spectacle of the Games arrives.

Few would disagree with the assertion that the Olympics, indeed any major event along these lines such as a World Cup or a Commonwealth Games, often adopt the form of a spectacle or a festival – a collection of people; cultures; nationalities and difference melded together for a definitive period that should allow for all sorts of positive companionship to play out. Speculating on the definition of the word "spectacle", Horne & Whannel provide a cutting (and, perhaps accidentally, vehemently political) classification on what it might constitute in the sporting sense. This arrives via the following, when they try to dissect various interpretations of the term – citing a work by Anne-Marie Broudehoux in the process.

> 12 "The first, derived from the Roman Circus, is that it was a mere distraction with the purpose of political control, and the second, derived from Guy Debord, is that it performs an ideological role in consumer capitalism. So in Leftist critical discourse the term is, almost inevitably, weighed down with strong connotations of negativness and irredeemability. Broudehoux (2007) argues that 'Beijing's spectacular Olympic preparations have in many ways acted as a propaganda tool and an instrument of pacification to divert popular attention away from the shortcomings of China's rapid economic transformation, accompanied by rampant land speculation, corruption and uneven development.' So spectacle becomes associated with oppression and control, and can be utilised to mask poverty and social exclusion."

Therein, we find a tremendous amount of theory on these events being used as masking agents regarding either what the ruling elite would like to bestow upon a nation or what is actually transpiring within the borders *of* a nation. Furthermore, we uncover a tremendous amount on how these festivals can be buried in the realms of the political, and not just any particular definition of the term "political", but the totalitarian and the border-line tyrannical. It would have been more pleasing had Horne and Whannel expanded on as to how "political control" might be more precisely defined within a context of speaking about Roman Circuses, but the crux of what is being explored here is disturbingly applicable to London 2012 with regards to diverting, not just domestic opinion, but potential overseas opinion with regards to portraying everything as being perfectly fine within the confines of Great Britain.

We are informed in the same work by Horne and Whannel that Karl Marx, in his seminal 1867 book *Das Kapital*, wrote briefly about how Capitalism (the ideology he loathed and sought to undermine) advances off the back of social disasters. We are reminded of a very acute, very specific passage from the text wherein Marx informs us that [13]"The shock doctrine [is] a philosophy of how political change can happen and be brought about". It will not, I hope, be lost on many people that the summer prior to London 2012 essentially saw London burning much in the same way Los Angeles did in 1992 shortly there*after* the '84 games. These were riots which spread throughout a nation gradually being torn apart, dismantled piece by piece if you will, as lawlessness and anti-social behaviour prevailed more and more during a radical shift to the Left in policies pertaining to numerous things, including policing.

By the time these riots had spread beyond London, they began to lack political character and started to resemble mere disturbances for sake of disturbances. In fact, there were stretches of the 2011 anti-social behaviour epidemic in parts of the city of London itself which were long since disconnected from the foundations of the event: that of the prior shooting of a black youth. It will not be lost, either, I hope, that the London Olympics took on a fresh complexion after these riots and after the insubstantial rhetoric about how they had been dealt with; cleaned up and that there was no longer a problem. London 2012 was suddenly the great shining beacon of a nation at one with itself; a country, and a city in particular, which was able to put the previous summer behind it and move on with the integration and socially harmonious plateau upon which it was predominantly formed in the first place.

The neo-liberalisation of the games in this sense, twinned with the desire to give London a "brand" name so as to increase tourism and utilise the venues for further monetary gain, was all one large papering over the cracks of a society on the brink of some kind of collapse into segregated republics through a deliberate decade-plus of policies designed to render the United Kingdom everything is never used to be.

Drawing on what Broudehoux wrote about, with regards to Beijing masking the reality of life in the nation of China, we witness London's own political Mafioso using the 2012 games as an agent to cover up two key items symptomatic of the journey that has seen

London reach the point whereby it is able to host an Olympiad of London 2012's nature. These might consist of any one of elderly people living alone and succumbing to the cold in the winter; the largely unmentioned and unnoticed cancelling of school nativity plays and Halloween themed decorations in school corridors to appease multicultural tastes or even the fact that the country, by and large, no longer has control of its borders nor what key legislation on a variety of things from the environment to agriculture might look like due to the being controlled from abroad.

The ideas on how one may utilise a spectacle as lavish and as commonplace as the Olympics to "divert" (the key verb) attention away from the wider social issues are here crucial, and are very much applicable to London 2012, where civic nationalism masks the tough realities of a broken society torn apart by Fabian reform and a genuine hatred of national identity. Horne & Whannel's own brief point at the end of the above draws our attention back to how spectacle can become associated with oppression and control; two things that are most certainly widespread in both British life and British political discourse at around the time of both before and after the 2012 Olympics, wherein opinion and independent thought detached from the ruling liberal elite's philosophy, irrespective of who you are, is met with derision and demonisation.

The author's ideas on how it can be utilised to hide the grimier and less glamorous aspects of a designated country, or city, ring true with the sordid spectacle London was and the various situations that have arisen out of the social politic the ruling parties have pursued. The fact something happening in the United Kingdom can be linked as easily as it can be here to a nation such as China speaks more for our own decline than is does for a city such as Beijing's ascent.

PART 3:
THE MULTICULTURAL AGENDA IN ACTION

THE INTERNATIONALIST INFLUENCE

To be of the opinion that the choice to hand the 2012 Summer Olympics to London was the exclusive result of some careful deduction and long, drawn out thinking – the likes of which eventually saw a delegation of forward thinking and respected intellects reach the conclusion that London stood head and shoulders above its meagre rivals, is fallacy. Those who decide such matters are, of course, the International Olympic Committee - an organisation we have already briefly looked at as being a group synonymous with affluence and exclusivity. The idea that the process to choose a host city is, in any way, surgical or precise can be quite easily disproved.

In furtherance to this, and despite what those responsible for the Games, embedded in the liberal British political thinking characteristic of this century as they were, would have no doubt liked the British population to think, London's hosting of the Games did not necessarily prove them and their ideology correct. There is no correlation between one's city, or nation, winning the rights to host the Olympic Games (either summer *or* winter) *and* being in any way a pleasant, constructive society within which to live or that its government's ideology is in any way sound.

With regards to this International Olympic Committee, it is interesting as to how Lee felt compelled to donate several pages to criticising (something he was in a position to do the moment the evening of 6 July 2005 had passed) them. Specifically, as being this incompetent and actually quite shady organisation, whose failure to get their own house in order (following the revelations that broke in 1999 that the decision to give Salt Lake City the Winter Games were somewhat corrupt) is quite laughable when lined up against the contemporary mantra of the "Olympic Spirit" which they often seem so keen to be synonymous with.

The bidding process by the involved host cities itself is not the free, easy and generally communalised process of harmony and friendly competition you would expect from something Olympic themed or with the supposed Olympic ethic at its core. Moreover, it is reduced to a bawdy "grab and go" situation which might be more synonymous with a New York City trading floor, where men bellow their message across to a gawping telephone possessing entity weighing everything up that is being said and acting accordingly. For something designed to be as universal and joyous as the Olympic movement is, there is almost certainly an awful lot of backbiting and backstabbing.

Some of the more stunning admissions by Lee arrive via his depiction of what generally unfolded within the London camp during those fateful few days in Singapore in July 2005, when Britain was unfortunate enough to have won the rights to host the Games. These arrive in the form of how prone Lee admits to changing their minds delegates of the International Olympic Committee were at the twelfth hour of voting, and how the likes of England football captain David Beckham, not to mention Tony Blair himself, who flew in to help out personally, impressed voters so much that it may have swayed them come voting time.

This places us in an extraordinarily dangerous predicament whereby we are faced with the assumption that years and years of hard graft and intense thought other cities have put into their bids are quite casually brushed aside for spot meetings and lucky coincidences with brand names at the most important time of all: the very last thing that happens to you prior to the voting session.

Britain were fortunate in this sense that they had a world figure as prominent as leader Tony Blair was, not to mention one of the most famous; richest and recognised sporting personalities the globe has ever seen, in David Beckham. These two gentlemen in their respective contexts, both sporting and political, managed to make their mark in the impressionistic stakes at a time when they were most vital. France, by comparison, who were second to London's bid, were able to boast the likes of President Jacques Chirac and footballer Zinedine Zidane, but it was not enough. Prizes should be offered to those who could name each of the respective leaders of Russia; Spain and the

United States at that time, with additional bonuses for the being able to name each of their respective teams' national football captains.

Thus, we must acknowledge that the whole bidding process can too easily relegate itself into what is essentially a popularity contest, and must in no way be used as a measure as to the domestic successes of the host nation. As we have already seen in the earlier chapters, legacy and hosting the games as a statement of national competence is a myth evident in numerous twentieth century examples. In the cases of Germany 1936 and the Soviet Union 1980, these nations plummeted from being a superpower with a feared reputation and an ability to host the Games to collapsing under the weight of their own portentous political ideology in a matter of a few years.

London was not the right choice because it could host the best games; moreover, it had at its core a rigid group of people who were more determined to grab the Games so that they may further their political beliefs than their rivals.

Lee offers us an insight into what Blair was thinking at the time of the Greek Games, held in the summer prior to London's announcement as victors, in what might be read into as an initial step in coining the idea to develop the Olympic project for political gain. This was at a time when it was already obvious to several others of his ilk that it might benefit the politic of the Left immensely were Britain to actually win the right to host it:

1 "There is no doubt Tony Blair was impressed by the Athens Games. He saw for the first time, first hand, how the Olympics could capture the imagination of a country and how they can bring about massive change."

Lee tries to mask the true intensions of what the London 2012 project was all about with a recounting of some ideas about domestic infrastructure, with particular attention to new airports; roads and tram stations - as if London needed any of that on top of what it had. But the crux of what is being preordained here is not an Athens travel infrastructure a city like London should be jealous of, but a sense of accomplishment and achievement inherent in how the Greeks took to hosting the Games – something which, if executed correctly back in Britain were they to have the chance, might enable the very makeup of Britain to move into new realms and in the irreversible multi-cultural direction those involved wanted to take it.

Away from this, Lee maintains that there was "something in the air" on a particular night in Athens around the time of Blair's visit – something which coincided with Kelly Holmes winning her now famous track gold medal after having come from behind to take first place on the line. It is a moment that is actually used to conclude a promotional video by the name of "*The Magic of London*", used during the official presentation the night of the bidding. What is asserted by Lee is that what was in the air was a strange, mystical quality which caught what Holmes was doing and injected it into the London bid as a whole; there was something about seeing Holmes roar on towards the line from a position of third or fourth to take gold. Much like the bid itself, things were creaking and it looked like London may not win at all – the bid had had its day and it was not to be. Suddenly, there is a second wind, and from nowhere the outsider surges forward to grab the prize.

The euphoria of Holmes winning was evident amongst British supporters, who were there with their Union Jacks and waving them frantically – something which only reiterated the commitment and passion for Olympic sport Britons have. The presence of Blair (he was the only world leader from any of the bidding nations to attend Athens 2004) and the fact all the right names from the International Olympic Committee were watching on from the stands at this precise moment gave London's bid that much needed boost when it came to those who mattered most to reach their decisions.

Three distinct people become relevant here, specifically: Nawal El Moutawakel; Sam Ramsamy and Frankie Fredericks. What they happen to share with one another in this particular context is set away from what they did to become such famous names in the first place, and it arrives in the form of each of them being members of the International Olympic Committee at the time of London's Singapore triumph. Prior to being members, El Moutawakel was a Moroccan runner in the 1980s; a woman whose achievements were made notable for the fact she is a Muslim and became quite renowned for what she achieved *because* of her nationality; gender and religion. Ramsamy is black and made his name as a fierce critic of the Apartheid rule which dogged his home nation of South Africa during the twentieth century, while Fredericks is likely he whom needs the least introduction of the three save for his impressive medal tally in both Commonwealth and Olympic meets. He too is black, and was a hugely successful Namibian sprinter.

This trio, a mixture of blacks and Muslims; people of varying faiths and nationalities, were officials of the International Olympic Committee charged with visiting the cities bidding to host the Games during the tenure of London's own attempt, and their contribution to London ultimately winning that bid must not go unnoticed. Indeed, a photograph of their meeting with Tony Blair at 10 Downing Street is depicted even at around the halfway mark of Lee's book, and is certainly viewed as something which was significant. We garner this from being told of how the visit was competently tailored so as to impress these delegates sent from afar with the task of remonstrating over whether London was up to the challenge of hosting duties. The fact that each of these three bodies, epitomised politically and ethically as they are, managed to find something in Blair, on top of seeing something in a city that had become what it had become, is surely stark enough evidence to suggest that there was something behind

London 2012 being the politically minded and politically motivated event it was.

That we can have this coalition of black Africans; Muslims and anti-apartheid campaigners fall so easily into line with the Blair ideal fuelling the Olympic bid, and witness them find allegiances in him as easily as they did so that Britain would eventually get the Games, should be viewed as revealing. This is due to the fact that they were, we must understand, meeting with a decrepit and deeply Anglophobic premiership who had already implemented upon a population political philosophies which covered an array of different departments and institutions - the likes of which the nation had never previously seen the like.

The relevance of going out of one's way here to make a point to mention the South African Apartheid rule is due to the uncomfortable fact that its synergy in recent times with a broader platform of social reform in Great Britain. While ultimately unconnected, most who purport to have been against the aforementioned white supremacist South African dictatorship it often seems carry with them this veiled hatred of the rest of the white Western world as well.

One reason for this may be down to the fact that Great Britain's most prominent Prime Minister during the reign of this regime was Margaret Thatcher; somebody who, as will be explored in the next few chapters, seemed to be somewhat sympathetic of the ruling group in her aversion to ban South African imports or even place the sorts of sanctions on the country which would undeniably hurt them. Hatred for apartheid somehow carried over to Britain at the time of both its own termination and Blair's ascent to the hilt of Labour.

Backing Nelson Mandela in the 1980's during the final few years of his life in prison, and campaigning for his release, seemed to synchronise with a wider desire to social reform in one's own country. The new age revolutionaries who were young enough in the 1970's to recall the large scale social reform which characterised Harold Wilson's government were old enough by the time of his release to occupy all the major positions in most of Britain's institutions, ranging from education to justice to politics and Blair's coming to lead the Labour Party in 1994 fell into perfect symmetry with Mandela's ascent to President of South Africa that same year. The fact that Mandela was a guest of honour at Labour's 2000 conference should come as no surprise those previously ignorant of it.

The issue of the South African apartheid regime and the topic of Nelson Mandela himself arise again when the time comes to depict Tony Blair's contribution to the Singapore presentation in 2005, with Lee telling us that he...[2]"...brought a message of support from Nelson Mandela, quoting the former South African president saying that he could not think of a better place than London to unite the world." The glaring question here is as to what Nelson Mandela even has to do with any of this in the first place away from the preceding ideas. It would, of course, be true to say that the man had a history of being involved in sporting triumphs which were designed to go hand in hand with the encouraging of integration and nationwide diversity.

The 1995 Rugby World Cup was South Africa's own version of this, a global event which carried with it socio-political undertones as a politic was furthered by a leader who wanted to build a very different nation to the one he had recently inherited; seeing said sporting event as a wonderful means to do so. But did Mandela's opinions on where the 2012 Olympics should be really matter anymore than, say, the Prime Minister of New Zealand's?

Turning to London's rival bids, the respective Spanish and French bids for the cities of Madrid and Paris, there is evident glee in *The Race for the 2012 Olympics* when the time comes for Lee to dismiss both of them. In spite of Western Europe's closer contemporary diplomatic and sovereign ties, something which we are told should lead to a greater "European" identity and sense of belonging – the refutation of nationalism for continentalism, there is room for Lee to exhibit a mite of the former in his written scorn for these two places and what they hoped to achieve. This is for the fact that they were, after all, standing in the way of London's success and were the chief rivals to Britain's attempt at hosting the Games if we set aside Moscow and New York as present to merely make up the numbers.

One notable area of repudiation of the rival bids is found his treating of their respective short films - pieces designed to instil into the watching International Olympic Committee voters the desire that they may select their particular city for hosting duties; notable for the fact it is more broadly linked to the overall tone of both the London bid and the actual execution of the 2012 Games themselves. Chiefly, it is viewed that Madrid and Paris made too much of what they were and what everybody already knew them for. It is, in Lee's opinion, that endless shots of conventional locations; stereotypical iconography and cultural items synonymous with the place in question are not good enough. Gone are the days when compositions of rich food and bottles of wine constitute as a means to convince the world that France might make for a good host city; gone, too, is the ridiculous assumption that endless shots of beaches and flamenco dancers put to guitar music should do for Spain's credentials in the hosting stakes.

This is, of course, in perfect synchronisation with earlier admissions on how it was important for Britain to establish to the suits of the International Olympic Committee that Britain had shed everything that it was for the past several hundred years and was now the benevolent god-parent of the planet; the Schindler's ark for the third world, of whom were oppressed in their homelands because no one there bothered to carve out a decent society or civilisation in the centuries of time they had to do so.

But do recall how this specifically anti-British tract was temporarily suspended for the best and the brightest of British culture when the time came for the visit of a handful of International Olympic Committee delegates in 2004, during which specific trips to each of the bidding cities was carried out. At Buckingham Palace, the Queen hosted banquets with sparkling Sussex wine rather than the French (the rivals) red equivalent; the meal itself was traditional British roast, etc. – all the time promoting this quasi-nationalistic rhetoric of how good old Britain and what characterised it for so long are what make it Great. It is nauseating to say the least.

After having dismissed Madrid and Paris, Lee turns his attention to London's video, entitled *"Magic of London"* – something constructed to be specially screened to the delegates casting the votes at the final bidding stages in Singapore in-between one of the British spokespersons trying pitching London's credentials. Much is made of this in Lee's account of how London won the bid, for the simple reason that two of London's big rivals, in Paris and New York City, had at their disposal two men, in Luc Besson and Steven Spielberg, who had accepted the call of duty to represent their nations in trying to bring the Olympics to them via the process of filmmaking. In spite of their own best efforts in utilising these moguls, London, sporting a film spearheaded by a virtual unknown heralding from a sleepy town in the north of England, triumphed.

Magic of London is only around three minutes in length and is generally set up to try and 'sell' London to the outsider or foreigner who might want to frequent it. Its aesthetic sees it stick to short, sharp cuts of various things from all walks of life to a harmonious overture of music. These compositions range from shots of its famous iconography to the Royal Family to everyday people smiling for the cameras. It has a pitch-perfect blend of that tacky, although slickly done, touristic quality most videos of this ilk possess alongside a genuine feeling that its maker is not actually trying to 'sell' anything to anyone at all, and is merely creating a love letter to the place they adore.

The film's more obvious problems lie with the fact the politic of the London 2012 Olympics was what it was: to endorse and encourage the creation of an entirely multiracial, multicultural Utopia where both the very definition and the very concept of a "Britain" would be redefined. London is, as per one of the film's numerous graphics quite candidly laying bare the project's overall politic, a "home for every nation", and it wants you to understand this over images of three children of distinct racial types holding hands and dancing in a circle.

It is worth mentioning here that the song overlying the images is entitled "Now We Are Free", and was originally composed by German composer Hans Zimmer for the 2000 film *Gladiator*. The significance is two-fold, for firstly the very name of the piece is designed to conjure up that sense of freedom or emancipation – that being let go from a form of imprisonment or slavery which, for some years now, the domestic Left have always seen as synonymous with Britain and its closed minded institutions: the criminalisation of homosexuality and their inability to marry; the strict attitudes towards drug control; the lack of human rights for criminals; the fact no theistic lifestyle away from Christianity had any kid of foothold in domestic life and the idea that procreating with someone of a differing ethnicity was frowned upon or seen as potentially "rebellious".

Secondly, being largely synonymous with a film as hugely successful as Gladiator was, the music succeeds in subliminally reminds people what can be achieved through a process of homogenisation and inter-cultural international efforts – Gladiator itself being a film with an enormous amount of recognition internationally for being such an international effort. When one observes the varying backgrounds and nationalities of the director; composers; cast; directors of photography and where the funding came from, etc. we see a visible connection between each of these different kinds of people combining to create something millions enjoyed.

The film darts along at a pace depicting each of the things which, as per its name, it considers renders London, or the United Kingdom more generally, a terrific place. We shoot from shots of centre court at Wimbledon to Trafalgar Square to the Red Arrows mid-air by way of the famous London Marathon to the changing of the guard. This is, of course, all fine and perfectly in sync with what might come to mind when viewing London through a Conservative lens, but the Leftist dimension of what the Games were is evident when we observe that the sweeping compositions of the food reveal little but sub-continental cuisine; that Concorde, once the pinnacle of Anglo-spherical engineering before it was decommissioned, and in spite of its presence in the feature, no longer flies; that David Beckham's famous free-kick against Greece in 2001 was at his then-home stadium of Old Trafford in Manchester, and not in London for the fact Wembley was being redeveloped to encompass architecture more representative of inclusivity; that the version of "*Now We Are Free*" overlying the piece is sung in a language meant to have more in common with Aramaic or Arabic than anything synonymous with Britain.

Away from the *visual* qualities of the presentation, Lee writes about the oral ones; the likes of which were put across to the watching officials within the bidding chamber itself. Crude as it may look, I will list them here, as it would be impossible to tackle them individually but for their similarity in tone and politic.

> 3 "We also paid attention to diversity and so
> we had a good mix of Olympic athletes,
> Paralympic athletes and people from different
> communities and cultures. This was a chance
> to start getting the messages across that
> would carry all the way through to Singapore
> [where the winning bid was announced]:

legacy, diversity, regeneration, government support and passion for sport. These were to become our key themes."

4 "To the surprise of many IOC members and the assembled media, more than a third of London's 100 strong delegation was made up of children from East London schools, 30 kids from 28 different ethnic backgrounds. They had been brought to Singapore as an embodiment of London's multicultural society."

5 "...Denise Lewis walked confidently up to the lectern. Her presence as a black female athlete at the heart of the London presentation team contrasted sharply with a Paris show dominated by white men in suits."

6 "Each is from East London, a community that will be touched by the games. They are a multicultural mix of two hundred nations representing the youth of the world, families from every continent, practising every religion. What unites them is their love of sport, London and the dream of bringing the Olympic Games to our city."

As is evident, these ethics from both Lee's book on how London won the games; admissions from the people behind the Games themselves, as well as what was uttered directly to those in the presentation chamber during the discourse over why certain cities would be superior to others as hosts, pertain exclusively to issues of multiculturalism and everything that comes with it. This last quotation, uttered by Sebastian Coe at the Singapore presentation ceremony as the cities did their utmost to convince the delegates of their unique qualities, followed the on stage presentation of around a dozen children of evident different backgrounds; the very ones spoken of at the beginning of the quotation. The intense fondness for a mixture of nations, two hundred we are told, different religions and people from essentially each of the five continents is a stark admission.

These citations remind us that the bidding team's core mantra was always a sense of diversity and cultural variety, the essence of Olympism without the concept that everybody should have a home to return to once the circus has finished. What is not admitted, nor ever explored, is how destructive these policies have the potential to be. The opening quotation, written about events of around a year prior to July 2005, confirms how evident the New Labour politic pertaining to attitudes about race and nation was in the project from such an early stage.

Touched upon very briefly earlier on, sporting spectacles, if geared towards the right people and executed in a particular way with the right results occurring, can have an immense influence on the country within which it is all happening as well as its inhabitants. The earlier examples pertained to Cathy

Freeman running at Sydney 2000 and the Canadian Ice Hockey team who, at Vancouver in 2010, swept the country up in a nationalistic fervour in their conquering of the United States in the gold medal match that any ideas that the Games themselves ought not have even been there, vanished.

Horne & Whannel make the brief, yet observant, remark that major sporting events can be both exploited and moulded into spectacles which go a long way in reshaping how domestic policy on how the citizens of that nation might live. They can be small in scale, with former Scottish first minister and leader of the Scottish National Party Alex Salmond's unfurling of the Scottish flag at the moment of compatriot Andrew Murray's triumph in the 2013 Wimbledon men's singles final being such an instance. The reason for this, of course, was due to the Scottish independence referendum being barely a year away from occurring. But as we have seen, it usually manifests itself in something far bigger and can be seen in any number of instances from Berlin 1936 to London 2012 by way of the 1995 Rugby World Cup, which was essentially Nelson Mandela's advertisement to the world that a post-Apartheid Premiership of blacks and whites existing harmoniously under the nickname of the "rainbow nation" was now in force. Therein, the authors speak of the opportunities that arise with regards to social reform, but also pay homage to how some sporting events lean towards unifying the world as an individual place and, although they do not quite put it in this fashion, therefore free of the burdens of nationhood and ethnic and cultural identity.

> 7 *"Today, not only are the Olympic Games an enormous lever for moving public policy and uncorking infrastructural investment...they are also a major contributor to the conception of the world as one place. Sports mega events...provide one of the means by which identity is constituted and reconstituted in the modern world."*

As the first decade of the twenty-first century transitioned into the second, the world powerhouses in the United States and the European Union were at loggerheads with the country of Russia, led by Vladimir Putin. Two years after the debacle of London 2012, the Winter Olympics were held in the Russian city of Sochi, in what was certainly a jump in ideological terms in that one was an Olympic project fuelled by a very precise sort of Blairite anti-nationalism to an Olympic meeting overseen by a man the rest of the first-world despised for the reason he actually exuded genuine conservative philosophies. The disconnect between the East and the West intensified when the Ukrainian revolution of February 2014 occurred and disagreements over Ukraine's trade and political future led to questionable election results; annexations and separatist movements forming in regions that were beyond *either* side's control. More broadly, Russia stood in the way at this time of both the

Western desire for the kind of global hegemony epitomised in the domestic policies of many western European governments and the founding principles of the European Union.

An observant article written in the aftermath of the opening ceremony to the Sochi Winter Olympics tries to get to the bottom as to why a particular giant model snowflake did not open correctly at the very beginning of the ceremony in what was otherwise a flawless show. It is here we must recall the nucleus of our last Horne & Whannel observation, regarding the idea (or "conception") of the world as one place and the means by which identity is 'reconstituted in the modern world'.

Citing the issue of globalisation, and trying to define this new era of freedom of movement between European states being in sync with the Blairite approach to immigration generally, as the fuel required to build a borderless utopia wherein the populous are each as indiscriminate as one another, the writer reminds us of the joint effort by those in the United States and Europe to continually interfere in the affairs of Syria and Libya and how Putin often acted to prevent such a thing. Spink reminds us that Putin, in... 8"...supporting the remaining independent Nation States in the Middle East from total annihilation and colonisation by this new globalised warrior class that foments local ethnic unrest into the next war zone", had thwarted the plans of the world's ruling elite to meddle where they should meddle not.

Speaking of the malfunction at the very beginning of Sochi's ceremony, Spink asks as to whether this was [9] *"...failure or fearless independence?"* for the reason that these iconic Olympic rings in a row of five represent each of the five world continents, and epitomise, in this author's view, [10] *"...the Olympic dream of a world united as one big happy family through the noble pursuit of sporting prowess, honest competition within the rules of the game and the sharing of celebration, festivity and much partying"*. When four of the five open and the last remaining ring stays closed before the ceremony moves on to the welcoming of the teams, we observe that in order for the Euro-American led desire to create pawns of mankind under one flag; anthem and unified territory spreading from world coast to coast, they ultimately need the consent of *all* territories. As Spink puts it,

> 11 *"...the architects of the New World Order (plan) to link all five continents of the world in their design...it will not work if one continent is left hanging... Did (Putin) make a rather clever gesture to confirm that he is not going to play their game?"*

If there was a sense that the British project of mass-immigration; diversity and multiculturalism was failing in some sort of way, the London 2012 Olympic Games sought to lay it to rest with a spectacular show of unity; solidarity and celebration of what we have only been for a mere speck of time in the grander scheme of historical things. As is stated in one of many works available on the issue of the Olympic Games and their social and economic ramifications, with regards to the building of sporting arenas, [12] *"Iconic stadium construction is about flagging transnational places and creating symbolic capital to attract middle and upper class visitors."*

It would not at all be inaccurate to classify Britain, or specifically London, a "transnational" place, while the attempt at reinventing the part of London where the main Olympic site was based and built might be read into as an instance of trying to bring people otherwise completely disconnected to a certain locale, *to* a locale. In this case, middle and upper class visitors to what was, ultimately, a stretch of scrubland in East London before the dreams of shopping malls and track and field sports arenas began to formulate.

Unlike previously, the Blairite hierarchy of Livingstone; Brown; Jowell et al., not all of them Members of Parliament because not all of them need to be, saw the Labour Party become more preoccupied with building and inducing recognisable iconography. The construction of a number of Dubai-like skyscrapers, such as The Shard, in Britain's capital could be read into as a further instance of Islamification through structure and iconography in a city which had already seen many millions from the Islamic world bestowed upon it anyway.

We looked at how the building of the rainbow-like arch atop Wembley stadium proudly stood in for the old, antiquated and wholly imperialistic two towers - this being Labour's first dabbling into the waters of sport as a means of political gain but more recently, the creation of the Olympic Stadium as this cathedral of multi-cultural; multi-racial; multi-faith rule was merely the natural step forward after having dismantled everything Britain was for so long.

We are reminded, once again, of Paul Jones' writing, cited in Horne & Whannel, that much of the above pertains to what was written in his 2006 work *The Sociology of Architecture and the Politics of Building*, wherein it is suggested that architecture in recent years has...

> 13 "...become an increasingly significant expression of diverse collective identities. Whilst landmark buildings were once a central way of 'expressing and developing the national code', Jones notes that they are now increasingly sites of symbolic conflict and competition over identities. In what he considers to be a post-national context, architecture can provide a cultural space for new identities to be expressed and contested."

Feeding off the meticulous 1936 attempts by Hitler and his German architects to create the perfect setting for an exhibition of racial and cultural supremacy, wherein those of the world and the citizens of Germany whom were invited were forced to observe, we observe that

Coe; Blair and their own team can now stand to be accused of inducing an equally politicised arena for their own more contemporary means.

FAST GIRLS, LOOSE MESSAGES

Propaganda is vital to the moulding of both public feeling and thought on an issue which is close to the hearts and minds of those running a society. The process has manifested itself in a variety of different ways down the decades, the predominant medium of the poster of the nineteenth century, where Uncle Sam or some such entity reminded the onlooker that he "...wanted YOU", eventually giving way to what constitutes as propaganda now: namely, just about anything from television advertisements to television soaps; from comics you see in your newspaper to your standard postage stamp.

In June 2012, a derivative, yet passable, sports movie centring around track and field athletes from Great Britain struggling with their lives; loves and one another directed by someone you had not heard of and using a formula so well worn that it made *The Needles* look like they were designed, was released. Its cinematic run and the periodic stumbling upon it through the means of post-watershed digital television should have been the last that we ever heard of Regan Hall's *Fast Girls*. Yet this incredibly infiltrative sports picture, released just prior to the commencement of the London Olympic Games and existing at the peak of its cinematic run from around the time of the Games' more immediate beginning, lives on as a bare knuckled exemplar of what contemporary political brainwashing looks like when it is green lit by those in charge of the society they are running and executed by those acting under orders who otherwise think they are contributing to a noble cause.

Set in London in 2011, the film follows Shania Andrews: a black woman in her twenties who dreams of making it within the domains of sprinting excellence. How far away she is from attaining that dream is epitomised in the crude cut from second-hand footage of famous track stars crossing the winning to the less glamorous surroundings of a municipal shed beside a ropey running track somewhere on a scrubland.

Following some success at a regional track and field meeting, she is invited to the headquarters of the Great British track and field administration, where hard training and rigorous routines snatch the humble newcomer out and away from their more grounded communal circles, and into the big league of state funding. Here, she meets the equally young and opportunistic Lily James - the daughter of a Sebastian Coe-like figure who was a medallist for Britain at an unspecified Olympic Games in the 1980's.

As one thing leads on to another, and tensions are strained with the inclusion of both a love rival in physio Bradley James' character and the fact they are from opposing sides of the class spectrum, makeshift team leader Noel Clarke must rally them into a four woman relay team for the world championships later that summer once Andrews has met and bonded with two more runners at the training centre.

The piece, cack-handed and imitative though it is, although often quite good value in that trashy way films such as Fast Girls can be when they are made with a sense of energy and style lacking in, say, a *Rocky* sequel, is barely much more than a calling card for its producers and writers. Its quite patent mistakes, in having Spanish athletes run under the competitive abbreviation "SPA" instead of the painstakingly obvious "ESP"; in having the film conclude in the summer of 2011 after beginning in November of that same year; of featuring a scene whereby the coach may learn of just how good the Americans are because they have conveniently uploaded the footage of their relay handovers to the Internet for him to see, is reminiscent of what ham-handed B-movies made with foul intensions and propagandist purposes might look like.

The reason for this was because it was an incredibly unsubtle piece of reformist propaganda which represented everything that would later come to be so wrong about the London Games themselves. At its very core is a tale about someone who, ambitious as they are, must come to learn that in order to succeed as a citizen of modern inclusive Britain, one must be willing to suspend any allegiance to Britain's past and embrace the common core of what London and most British cities now epitomise: diversity and variety.

The overarching relationship in the film is one between four female sprinters, the half-caste Andrews;

the rich, upper class white girl played by James; the all-black Belle Newman, played by Lashana Lynch, and a second half-caste girl named Trix. Furthermore, Andrews' obvious status as a rookie within these competitive circles, and Newman's role as a veteran undergoing her own individual narrative as this person going for one last attempt at a World Championship gold medal, rounds things off. The ingredients to the piece are thus a mixture of diverse women, of varying ethnicities, who are young and old and rich and poor being thrust together so as to triumph over long odds.

The group will, throughout the film, compete against other runners and national relay teams that are of a more familiarised stock whilst promoting a series of radical social democratic policies pertaining to diversity and multiculturalism. Distinctions are made between Britain's diverse squad of four and a nation such as Ukraine's all white, and therefore inferior, team of girls, while Spaniards look like Spaniards; Italians look like Italians and Russians like Russians. Nativism in this regard loses, but loses more specifically to the diversity of Great Britain, which is stronger because it is a mixture of the brightest and the best; the team itself only periodically losing to the United States, upon whose national model, in a cultural and ethnic sense, the United Kingdom (indeed, the continent of Europe) is now openly based.

Used for po-faced dramatic effect is the fact that the two athletes whom like one another the least, in Andrews and James' character, run the final two legs.

They are thus forced into facing the reality whereby one must hand to, and therefore take from, the other as a race enters its most crucial stage. This ludicrous scenario, practise of which would not occur in life, and of which is designed to act purely as faux-drama within an internal filmic sense, is supposed to highlight two things: firstly, the power of what can happen when two opposites are eventually forced into attracting. More specifically, this is the process of fighting to overcome initial differences and coming together to embrace inclusivity once the initial problems are conquered. Secondly, just how destructive, even bigoted and backward, older philosophies of repelling those not of your sort in a class or racial sense can be when you let them overcome you.

The revolving of the film around a relay team in the first place is novel, in so much there is an intrinsic focus on the 'team' as an item of narrative spectacle; the fate of the 'team' is what matters in the film and has become the focus by the time of the final race. Films such as *Fast Girls* have a happy habit of centring around the individual as a device for depicting sporting drama and epiphany: the derivative way in which Paul Bettany wins in *Wimbledon*; the manner in which the aforementioned Rocky Balboa might come back from a bad loss to triumph over a foe to whom he would ordinarily lose inside ninety seconds; the way a drunk and sufferer of post-traumatic stress syndrome, born out of exposure to World War One, rises to take on two of the greatest golfers in history in *The Legend of Bagger*

Vance. With regards to *Fast Girls*, 'group' replaces 'individual'; with diversity and the tolerance those within the team come to understand is needed for a functioning unit to propel themselves through a London, indeed a Britain, which is changing quite dramatically.

Before we get to the point where the team win their coveted gold medals, we witness Andrews initiate a love affair with that aforementioned physio, who is white and is thus one half of a mixed race relationship. Indeed, the concept of a mix race relationship seems to be buried within the confines of the track and field movement anyway and thus we can only deduce the pursuit of excellence in track and field to be further-still mired in that of the liberal-left.

This is no surprise, for excellence within these disciplines requires one to be of a younger disposition and younger people generally lean towards liberal views. Furthermore, there is a long tradition of the pursuit of athletics attracting a certain class of individual more attuned towards the politics of the left; specifically, the working class, whose tendency to lean more towards Green orientated views combined with their fondness for a healthy lifestyle, which may or may not include early morning jogs and visits to a local gymnasium. London 2012 was, of course, driven by its poster child Jessica Ennis; herself the product of a mixed race marriage and who in 2013 married a white gentleman.

This is in perfect synchronisation with Mohamed Farah, whose Somali roots see him a black African but whose wife is white. The spectacle of Mohammad and his wife, complete with their children, was often made possible by each of them making frequent appearances on the running track following one of Farah's triumphs. This in turn allows the image to be used as a means to break into the minds of those watching an alternate way of finding kinship to the more traditional means of starting a family with one of your own.

But it is the heptathlete who appears to engage in that of the mixed race dynamic to relationships the most. Iconic Briton and leading name and voice behind the 2004-05 bidding project, a woman who was essentially a precursor to Ennis, Denise Lewis harbours a white husband, while renowned Canadian heptathlete Brianne Theisen-Eaton is white and was married to an African American at the time of the 2014 Commonwealth Games.

The final race itself, once finished, proceeds to initiate a montage of the various faces of those joining in the gold medal success from their various platforms – both at home and the stadium. This essentially consists of those of varying class and racial denominations, encompassing that of Andrews' black family; her ex-trainer, who is the white working class shopkeeper played by Phil Davis, and also that of the father of her ex-rival James, who watches on in full knowledge that he will go home to an ivory tower at the end of the evening where mostly everyone else will not.

The closing montage in this regard is a sweep through the Britain of the time and depicted the people those at the very peak of the Olympic project wanted congregating together to get behind those running for the Union Jack. The closing composition of the film, the four girls harbouring broad smiles as they occupy the race track holding said flag aloft behind them as they squeeze into shot, is a wonderfully politically driven piece of visual propaganda. The founding socialist concepts of the Olympic Games being a tie that binds people from varying class backgrounds together for two weeks of sporting excellence are evident here, the likes of which were borrowed and manipulated to encompass the accepting of Islam as permissible; the acknowledging of traditional men and women's roles being inverted and the smashing of the mixed-race taboo. Goebbels would have been proud.

THE SHAMBLES OF SPORT AND POLITICS COMBINING

14"...it is impossible to separate the Olympic Games from the broader social context of modern Britain. 7 July 2005 remains a tragic reminder of exactly that."

One of the more appealing aspects of events such as The Commonwealth Games; the various World Cups of world team sport, or even the Olympics themselves, is that, for a designated period of about two or so weeks, your country or a city in your country is the epicenter of the entire planet. That is to say, for a brief window the world descends onto a territory in a controlled and manufactured manner for specific reasons more broadly associated to sporting participation. This is usually a solid ninety percent of the experience – to have, where previously there was nothing of its sort, the various dresses; languages; cuisines; pastimes; customs; people and ethnicities come to where you live for very clear and controlled predetermined reasons with the view to enrich the experience of hosting the event in the first place. When the time comes for the sporting mega-event you happen to be hosting to conclude, everybody departs along with all the alien material that initially came and you go on being what you always were.

In many ways, such a thing used to be what made events such as the Olympic Games as special and unique as they were. A scenario along these lines is what *would* have made London 2012 as special as everybody only *thought* it was, were the London to which the world came stuck true to what it had always been *prior* to the Games. As is entirely evident, the world is already *in* London; the city itself had already been re-rendered such a melting pot of differing creeds, peoples and languages that the very concept of something foreign and exotic traversing to the city in 2012 was limited exclusively to the architecture not already present.

It is in this sense that the novelty of such an occasion, an occasion where you would genuinely see and hear different people; languages and fashions in your home during this festivity of sport, was largely detached from London 2012 as a concept of Olympic experience. There was a delightfully nostalgic article on the official website of FIFA (The Federation of International Football Associations), which alas I now cannot find and fear has been removed permanently, written by an Englishman who was only ten years of age when his country hosted the 1966 World Cup. Living and growing up in Sheffield, the son of a miner, the author wrote of his joy at being taken to a match at what was usually his home team's stadium of Hillsborough. He wrote of his awe at seeing two other countries playing one another; at how memorable it was to see two sets of fans otherwise alien to the venue and to just generally be amongst the focus of something foreign and irregular.

With regards to the Berlin Games of 1936, Hilton observes that there was a great deal of both confusion and disbelief on the faces of the German locals of the suburbia around the Olympic Stadium when Jesse Owens and the other black American athletes were first spotted walking around and getting to know the place. What these German citizens were doing is described by Hilton as "gawping" at something so totally alien, that it left them stunned enough to react how they did.

But there were other aspects, or characteristics, to Nazi Germany's welcoming of the world for this two week stint in the summer of 1936: a brass band was on order to play the national anthems of each of the competing nations upon their arrival, with the flag of the respective nation going up simultaneously as they would disembark from the docks following a long boat journey. This actually resulted in numerous renditions of "God Save the King" for when the likes of India and Australia arrived, an anthem which of course belongs more directly to a nation Germany were at war with not twenty years earlier and would be again in just three.

Furthermore, each of the countries were allowed their own set menu – there was a desire to know what each of the competitors ate and a thirst for this premise of the world arriving in Berlin, complete with everything they do back home, to arrive *with* them. If the competitors from Afghanistan did not want to have to eat pork because of their religious requirements, in

Germany of all places: the home of the bratwurst
sausage, then they were appeased. There was an
enormous amount of respect for those who were not at
all Aryan, or even remotely white, in the form of the
Japanese swimming and diving teams, whose
meticulous training regimes and thorough routines were
held in high regard by their German counterparts.

In 2012, British organisers did not need to appease
to Islamic eating customs, for they had been busily
doing it for the last few decades anyway; there was no
need to make a tremendous deal about the arrival at the
airports of the competitors, for people from all over the
world had been flying in and occupying various
London boroughs and residences for some time. There
was no need to loiter around the Olympic village in
order to see or hear something foreign or unfamiliar, for
there was so much of it already in abundance in the
city. We needed not to marvel at the skills of an African
long distance runner, for we had one running *for* us.
There was a strange, detached sense of simulacrum
about the world arriving in London for 2012: the
headscarf's adorning the female athletes of Bahrain
during the opening ceremony were not shocking; the
exotic dresses worn by the Ugandan women also during
said event would not have been out of place outside of
the stadium itself, while the sheer number of
individuals of varying racial and national makeup
adorning the sporting stage from varying continents just
seemed to feel at home. Whether you were from
Turkmenistan; Samoa or Peru, that incredible sense of a

cultural spectrum forging itself as the epicenter of a spectacle driven by a marveling at diversity was vacant.

Politics and sport should never mix, and yet are inseparable. Even during the *bidding* for the 2012 Olympic Games, a fight of which was largely fought between the cities of Paris and London, they could not remain apart. But it was these two cities, or perhaps their political leaders at the time of the bidding process in 2004, that appeared to be competing on an even greater keel away from the potential to host the ultimate in track and field competition. Just the year previously, Iraq was invaded out of the panic that erupted due to the fallout of September the eleventh 2001, when the United States was targeted by an Islamic terrorist cell in a series of coordinated attacks. The predominant forces involved in this invasion were the United States and Great Britain, with the rest of Europe and the developed world leading the call to avert an invasion.

The Americans; the British and the French have been inseparable from one another as a holy trinity of developed, free-thinking democracies ever since post-war Nazi Germany was divided into four separate pieces. The Soviet half of the East is largely irrelevant here, but the remaining half saw three separate thirds handed over to Britain, France and America, respectively. In 2003, it was the French, through President Chirac, who resisted supporting what was otherwise two thirds of this alliance represented by Bush and Blair when they rejected the idea of going into Iraq in pursuit of Saddam Hussein's weapons of mass destruction.

As a consequence, Lee reminds us of the political dimensions hovering over the decision in 2005 to award London the Games instead of Paris – ultimately insinuating that Blair's position to be in favor of an invasion was somehow rendered 'correct' because London won, and that it was that element which left Paris and Chirac without an Olympics for the fact he did not support what Blair supported in the disarming of Hussein.

This is, of course, fallacy, for how could the political dynamics of such a scenario transplant their way into the vast voting halls of a Singapore-set International Olympic Committee meeting? This is not to say that there should not have been a fear of this striking the people voting that day, for they were ultimately human-beings with their own thoughts and opinions, and it may very well have been the case that a number of IOC officials in that chamber had their own designs and thoughts on what should have happened regarding Iraq.

It is at this point that we must remember that the leaders and citizens of the world were largely *against* the invasion, and that the Singapore chamber was of course made up of a group of people epitomising the world over. On this evidence, Paris ought to have won quite comfortably. Then there is the issue of the American bid and the candidacy of New York City, which finished well below that of the French bid in

spite of America adopting the role of chief sabre-
rattlers to Hussein's demise. In fact, the Parisian bid did
extraordinarily well to see off both the Americans *and*
the Spanish when we observe the fact that Madrid
finished a close third behind the French, and that the
then-Spanish premier was in favour of the Iraq war.
The fact that London defeated Paris does not, of course,
mean that the Iraq war decades on was justified, nor
does it cement the idea that people are better off in Iraq
due to the invasion. What it does demonstrate,
however, is that politics and sport are frustratingly
inseparable and that any minute issue which rears up
between two countries can cause people to go looking
in all sorts of areas for larger meanings to an event
when there is nothing initially there.

It will not escape anybody over a certain age, nor
those more attuned than others to the recent history of
Great Britain, that the day after London won the right
to host the Olympics, the city itself was rocked by a
terrorist attack. This attack could not have come at a
more poignant moment. July the sixth and then July the
seventh: a pair of dates which will stand inextricably
locked together for the rest of time as the days London
was able to both celebrate as well as mourn its politic
of multicultural multi-racialist inclusivity - the joy of
the sixth could not of course have happened without it,
but in equal measure the tragedy of the seventh could
have been averted had the city not already been driven
by it. The event that was the 2012 Olympics could in no
way have brought the happiness and pleasure to the

millions of Londoners that it did without its politics,
but the people whom lost their lives on July the seventh
2005 would still be alive had it not been implemented
in the first place.

The sad fact is that the July seventh (only
colloquially referred to as "7/7", in lieu of America's
own "9/11") attacks were carried out by people
vehemently opposed to the politic of multiculturalism,
further-still in a place whose existence as a city
subscribing to the neo-liberalist economic model now
depends on it. They do not believe in a figure such as
Jessica Ennis acting as a role model for young women,
as young women do not need such things – who better-
a role model for anybody than that of their Prophet,
Muhammad, anyway? They do not adhere to the belief
in women [15]"confidentially striding forward" to match
the male gender in authority and discourse, at least not
in the same way Kelly Holmes did at the Singapore
presentation ceremony when the time came for her to
argue London's case to a stuffy auditorium full of
suited elderly men. Nor do they subscribe to somebody
such as singer Elton John, whose lifestyle is what it is,
playing a key role in bringing this festival of diversity
and tolerance to a city most of them have already
claimed as their own.

One must not in any way infer that there was some
sort of link between the actions of those who killed
both themselves, and dozens of others, on 7 July 2005
and that of the Olympic Games as a standalone event
which unfolded in London in the summer of 2012. This

is down to the fact that it would be foolish to believe that the people responsible for that fateful day in 2005 were of sound enough mind and reasoning to deduce all of: what Tony Blair represented, politically, and who he was; what London had now become, after centuries of it being what it was, and what the 2012 Olympics might come to epitomise when the time came to present twenty-first century London to the world as this haven of blacks; whites; Jews; Muslims; homosexuals; female boxers and male gymnasts who were apparently capable of celebrating its class divide.

What is important to the case here is that, on 11 August 2012, when Mohamed Farah crossed that finish line to complete the 5,000m event and win the gold medal, it offered a catharsis to millions of liberal-leaning commentators; academics and politicians that Muslims *could*, in fact, do Britain proud; *could* have the majority of the non-Islamic population get behind them and *were* able to engage in a celebratory spectacle involving both the Union Jack and a sense of achievement. Farah's gold medal, not to mention his later one in the 10,000m, was in this sense the most important of all the British gold medals at the 2012 Games; medals which blew the shame of July the seventh 2005 as this apparent epitome of a failed multicultural project away - replacing it with the glory of what multiculturalism is capable of doing for a nation, albeit on a sporting stage.

It is difficult to go through one's life without both hearing and reading a great deal about the British Prime

Minister of 1979 to 1990 Margaret Thatcher, and
depending on the source, not all of it is complimentary.
Here is not the place for any kind of real discussion on
the cavernous subject that-is both her premiership and
the political philosophies of the woman, although I will
touch on one particularly delicate issue with regards to
one of the more divisive Prime Ministers of all time:
that of the apparent soft spot she had for what was
happening in South Africa at the time of her
premiership, specifically the white on black segregation
characterised by the Apartheid system.

It was, in fact, this political stance that cost Great
Britain the Olympics in 1992, when a bid tabled in the
late 1980's essentially bottomed out because the
International Olympic Committee thought it wrong to
take the Games to a nation run by someone susceptible
to the views Thatcher possessed. Her philosophy in this
regard contaminated itself with a sporting context in
1986, a year in which Scotland's capital city,
Edinburgh, hosted the Commonwealth Games -
something which eventually saw the boycotting of the
event by a variety of predominantly black
Commonwealth countries who were protesting against
Britain's hosting it. Indeed, the Commonwealth Games
as an event, we must recall, was established on what are
regarded today as thoroughly racist principals, and had
to undergo its various name changes from being the
Empire Games as Britain effectively *lost* that of
possessing an empire in the first place.

In 1986, as it is today, the Commonwealth Games actually has England; Scotland and each of the British communities (extending to the Isle of Man) competing individually rather than as a unified team, but Thatcher, being Prime Minister of the United Kingdom, was seen as the *leader* of each of these dominions as a whole, and since Scotland fell within the constraints of this United Kingdom, various people saw it as an event and a locale embedded in what Thatcher believed. Due to her stance on what was happening to the black population of South Africa, best represented through her refusal to place sanctions on the nation of South Africa which would have eased the suffering of the Black population, and despite Scotland's population largely *sharing* these people's philosophies in rejecting Thatcher, nations such as Nigeria; Uganda and Ghana decided against attending.

The greatest instance of politics and sport combining as horrifically as is possible actually came when the Bermudan government only pulled their athletes out of the tournament *after* the opening ceremony, meaning that the would-be competing Bermudans would instead be facing the long flight home instead of pulling off what they had channelled all of their time and effort into for the last few years. We have already explored how people such as Farah; Ennis and Adams can be utilised as political pawns in their athleticism and ability to prove a philosophical point, but the Bermudans in 1986 were an antithesis of sorts with regards to this: the ultimate statement of *un-*

intent; the hammering home of sets of views their politicians had on an issue or an ideology, represented here by a *refusal* to take part instead of using their athletes to dominate the tracks and fields.

It is theorised by Horne & Whannel that boycotting sporting events actually has very little impact on events, irrespective of whatever cause it may be; that the games will go on regardless, and those who witness them will go on to remember more that of who *were* present, through their incredible athletic feats, rather than who were not because of some political statement someone attempted to make. But this was not necessarily the case in 1986, for even with the mere *presence* of a boycott looming, as Thatcher and the Royal Family clashed on the issue, the Games were hurt in an economic sense with people delaying purchasing tickets and several sponsors dropping out of supporting the event entirely. To appease the situation, athletes were again caught up in the crossfire of politics, and the dreams of two South Africans, runner Zola Budd and swimmer Annette Cowley, who were now competing for England on the grounds of nationality shift, were destroyed when they were dismissed from competing because of what was still essentially their link to South Africa.

Due to the fact that the 1984 Los Angeles Olympic spectacular scored the American economy large amounts of money, Britain were keen to obtain a similarly sized monetary windfall from Edinburgh. This dream ultimately fell short due to a variety of reasons, no less these political ones, which saw sponsors pull out of endorsing a sporting event which would go on to obtain too much political baggage. Prior to the Games, and with the situation desperate, organisers were reduced to skimming through British newspaper *The Financial Times* for potential companies who might lend a hand lest the competition be cancelled. One Robert Maxwell answered the call, but remained sceptical as to whether he could even save the Games from losing out on a profit – stating that were they to fall short, the surplus required to pay off the bill would almost most certainly fall at the feet of Thatcher. Despite stating that he had effectively broken the Games even, later reveals told a different story – in that he had left the Games with a large debt and the whole thing had been a bit of a fiscal disaster, and all down to the politics of it.

The notion of boycotting derives, like so many of our modern amalgamations of sports and politics, from that seminal sporting fortnight in 1936 in Berlin. The United States, toying with whether or not to send a team made up mostly of Jews and African Americans to a place where it was practically against the law to be either, seemed destined to boycott the event at a time when such things did not happen. In the end, they went, but were beaten into first place in the medals table for both the most gold's and the most overall. Thus, boycotting would at least have spared them the humiliation of actually losing to this monolith of a political force, who always maintained their citizens were superior for the fact they were whiter and now had the results sheet to prove it.

It is here, then, that we could essentially deduce that the notion of boycotting derives from a fear of losing; from a fear of being beaten by your rival or opponent – politically, racially or ideologically. This is far more evident with regards to the Capitalism/Communism dichotomy of the 1980's, likewise the Edinburgh boycott of 1986, where it was likely expected that athletes and swimmers from Thatcher's seemingly apartheid friendly Britain would trounce the athletes from the poorer, less developed black nations. The entire concept behind what were initially the Empire Games were, after all, set up to exemplify this very spectacle in the first place, and the likes of Uganda and their allies were not about to allow a late twentieth century equivalent happen at their expense.

Another unfortunate variety of this occurred in 1976, at the Canadian summer Olympics, when a showdown between the two greatest 1,500 meters runners in the world was taken away from audiences because of a boycott. Enraged that New Zealand were partaking in Montreal, African country Tanzania pulled their team out of going because the New Zealand rugby team (an otherwise completely detached entity) had recently toured Apartheid South Africa in what were often referred to as "rebel" tours when respective rugby and cricket teams did such a thing against common recommendation. This deprived the world of a race between New Zealander, and eventual gold medallist, John Walker and Tanzania's Filbert Bayi; a showdown between the world record holder and the gentleman who was considered to be the best in the world at the distance going into that summer.

Ideology contributing to boycotts was all but vacant at London 2012, for sake we were open to mostly everybody and everyone. There were no ill-feelings with regards to any country from any part of the world that caused anybody to boycott; no ties to places that enraged others, no 'one' ideology to upset a country enough for them to stay away. Our allegiance and strong, long term ties with the United States did not in any way see them threatening to pull out. Ties to Saudi Arabia, to the extent numerous Saudi funded mosques adorn various British towns, as well as to numerous other despotic Islamic nations, meant we were on good terms with them. Links to the European Union, of course, resulted in each of the European countries coming.

There was no need for an African country to stay away, nor a Latin American one. Israel did not have a problem with coming, nor Palestine – not even Russia, fragile and disconnected in political thinking as we were with one another, stayed away. This suggests an ideological imbalance within the British political spectrum; one, perhaps, of appeasement and conciliation wherein the world consists of everyone and everyone as well as the whole world can come to London. The lack of stonewall philosophies on a variety of differing issues could be argued as to being present. In its place is the taking time to seemingly embrace everything – something which allows dozens of nations the opportunity not to feel despondent towards us in any way. In a lot of ways, this is connected to the rooted nature of Tony Blair and his premiership, where cross-spectrum policies and a real desire to move into third way ideology, where nobody is seemingly left behind and where Thatcherism and democratic socialism can live side by side, drives proceedings: some of which were, unarguably, on show during London 2012.

STANDING ON CEREMONY - LONDON'S OPENING AND CLOSING GAMBITS REASSESSED

Opening ceremonies, in their modern form, are a recent innovation. The 'ceremonies' in the years before television would quite literally consist of a handful of speeches from top ranking officials and the welcoming out of the competing teams. These occasions were short and often concise, made so due there being such a small audience to appease and doubly so due to the fact there were never as many countries competing in the past as there are now. With the idea in mind that Berlin 1936 was the first Games to utilise the concept of both an Olympic torch relay *and* an Olympic flame burning throughout the event, we must also conclude that the ceremonies to the Olympic Games up until this point did not even need to run through the process of welcoming in a runner who would then light a cauldron.

The reason that the opening ceremonies of today largely consist of the extravagance and length that they do is for the fact television exists. Thus, both a vibrant and glamorous display of performance and spectacle is expected to be played out for the benefit of those possessing the modern equipment. As the television technology develops from black and white into colour; from mono to stereo; from standard definition to high definition and from two dimensions to three, so too do the opening ceremonies escalate in size; extravagance and expenditure – a forcing of the organisers to outdo the previous show whilst at the same time essentially be able to live up to the new technology millions of those watching at home have bought their screens to watch it on.

The ceremonies are ultimately superfluous, and exist entirely as an exercise in cultural exhibitionist muscle flexing whereby the host nation are able to show off to the watching world their ability to put on a spectacle. The majority of the ceremonies are designed to epitomise, or advertise, to the rest of the globe the essence, or perhaps 'quintessentiality', of the host nation; for instance, Russia's 2014 Winter Games opening traversed the viewer through the history of the country, from its humble icy beginnings, through to the modern post-Soviet era by way of anti-Tsarist revolutions; Sputnik rockets; industrialisation and Stuka sirens designed to encapsulate World War Two. Among the many ceremonies from history, China's 2008 opening laid claim to being the country responsible for inventing the compass, such are the stakes at presenting to watching worldwide audiences that sense of "national pride".

Much more recently, the occasions have attracted personnel from the world of film to oversee their direction – with Yimou Zhang and Daniel Boyle each respectively taking charge of the 2008 and 2012 ceremonies. In many ways, this push into the realm of cinema in this regard is in sync with the broader assertion that they exist in the first place for the spectacle of television, as the world veers into unparalleled dimensions associated with high definition screens and modernity that essentially allows us to take screens with us when we leave our homes.

The opening ceremony to London 2012 took place on Friday 27 July, and began on a gloomy yet humid evening at seven o'clock before concluding a few hours into the following day. It was divided into three separate thirds, that of performance; athlete introductions and what appeared to be an attempt at an outdoor rock concert. It was bathed in a plethora of electronic lighting; featured a range of various pieces of music and was held together by several eclectic items of performance.

That sense of cinema being at the forefront of the opening ceremonial spectacle actually arrived with its opening shot, a composition from a camera perched high above the River Thames on board a helicopter as it focused steadily on Saint Stephen's Tower whilst allowing for a background of bridges and cityscape to fill in. It is American director David Lynch who is largely credited with pioneering the being able to express within the confines of the cinematic frame the concept of an exterior surface clashing with interior reality. The 'book' example is his 1986 film *Blue Velvet*, which begins with your more idyllic suburban

American street harbouring white picket fences and smiling members of the emergency services. But away from the tranquillity, two insects tussle uncomfortably in the undergrowth via an unpleasant extreme close up, thus suggesting something less than perfect or more sinister once you delve beyond the surface sheen. Sure enough, as the film progresses, we watch a story about a young lead discovering that all is not well in his friendly neighbourhood American town.

As our camera here, on board the helicopter, flies forward, moving past The Palace of Westminster and the Millennium Dome, things become less familiar. By the time we have passed the banking sector of The City, with its tall buildings and cordial appearance, we are in the proverbial no-man's-land of uncharacteristic buildings and blocks of flats. This is before we reach the evening's venue, a large bowl of a stadium with its corners whipped up and curled over at the top so as to just about tower over those beneath them. This is it: we have reached what lurks beneath the surface of the city in an area of it that now sports structure where, previously, it was fittingly enough nothing but canal-side scrubland. Welcome to the setting for where the insects will duel, where a seedy spectacle of falsehood and misrepresentation will play out in ways that best epitomise what Britain is beneath the shrubbery of renowned landmarks that people around the world naively still associate with the United Kingdom.

It would, of course, be foolish to suggest that this was deliberate. Why, after all, would the British authorities in charge of the broadcast attempt to create a distinction as evident as this one is? Moreover, the said unbroken tracking shot revealed so much more than any preordained sequence could have done in that unique way things often can when they are unplanned; subliminally executed and that only later become evident when you review the material. It was, you might say, rather similar as to how British diver Tom Daley appeared to play such a large role in the pet-political project that-was-London 2012 without ever really quite centralising himself as one of the "faces" of the Games, not at least in that way the likes of Adams; Farah and Ennis did. When the time came in December 2013 for Daley to reveal himself as homosexual, there was that sense of two pieces of a jigsaw puzzle suddenly coming together.

Inside the venue, *Nimrod*, by Elgar, is warming the audience up into a state of fervent anticipation; a piece of music often synonymous with bereavement or perhaps the sadder occasions in life that are linked to remembrance and nostalgia. Might this be the 'death' of the older guard of what Britain once was? Was it a sweeping out of the outdated and a whisking in of the new? Peter Hitchens, in his scathing 1999 book on the philosophies of New Labour entitled *The Abolition of Britain*, makes a brief comparison between former-Chinese premier Mao Zedong's attempts to bury both an entire nation's rich history and its cultural traditions once in charge, and New Labour's attitudes towards the United Kingdom's own such things – best epitomised in the political philosophies of the Blair-led organisation.

Whether the presence of Elgar at the beginning was a greater representation of this or not, there was at least an opportunity to observe a time in this opening ceremony when England was a greener and calmer land; where our own picket fences, here brown, cordoned off cricket playing villagers from humbly dressed women appearing to gather water from our streams. This is a calmer, simpler England; people seem to move in slow motion. When a bowler partaking in the cricket match does not pick up the wicket he is appealing for, they merely get on with the game at the behest of an authority figure not on the end of any disrespect.

But this England seems strange and alien, even foreign; it does not register with anyone in the audience in the way that later, louder and more colourful sequences do. There is an unspoken embarrassment amidst those watching at the segment and it is deliberately underplayed by Boyle who knows this is not what people have come to see, nor what they will take away with them. In fact, the discomfiture is so intense that by the time the horse drawn carriages have arrived and white men in tops hats are about to stroll around the arena, we feel the need to self-censor by cutting to otherwise completely unrelated archive footage of rugby matches involving the home nations. When this is not utilised, we cut to mixed race choirs of young children singing in harmony in outdoor locations throughout the Kingdom.

What these men in hats and horse drawn carriages usher is another one of Britain's famous revolutions, the one of an industrial nature; led here by Kenneth Branagh as Isambard Kingdom Brunel, who quotes Shakespeare and initiates what is essentially a release from the white-skinned dominated 'green and pleasant land' aesthetic epitomising pre-Industrial Britain, with the tearing away of its grass and erection of chimneys and factories.

In what is ultimately a broadcast of four hours, with ample time, remember, set aside for the reams of athletes to enter the stadium later on, what is quite remarkable is that the ceremony only reaches its nineteenth minute when it eclipses the First World War. In doing so, it essentially conceals a lot of what preceded said conflict up to this very early twentieth century point in our history; some of which are: British colonialism, not all of which was murder and wrongdoing; a fantastic array of poets and writers; the establishment of a parliament and a number of inventors and their inventions which have done only good for the world. Whether or not it is apt to describe the decision to do such a thing as a "burying" of the past depends on the beholder.

Either way, and from this point onwards, the ceremony literally bounds through the twentieth century, really only the real passage of time in Britain's history it is in any way interested in depicting, with a verve and an energy that was very much lacking earlier on. Much of this derived from what time of day it was at the point it had reached this section, with artificial lighting taking over proceedings and allowing the later segments to look brighter and more colourful - various purples and blues complimenting one another to create a sea of vibrancy. Contrasted to the opening gambits, lit only by the white light of nature and not granted the steel and verve of later parts, by which time darkness had descended, these depictions of life and more contemporary British achievement are very much more energetic. This makes a lot of the propaganda more striking in this sense, events of which are already being broadcast into the homes and minds of those watching that have bought special televisions of the latest technological variety in order to see everything in the best quality anyway.

When the time does come to cover some of Britain's literature, it is melded in with a celebration of the National Health Service, itself is one of the great British socialist innovations and an institution for which the Labour Party of 1945 were responsible. This brief literary segment, somewhat inexplicably, focuses only on the various villains from certain children's books Britain has been responsible for. Even then, we are not treated to what may have been a physical incarnation of any character in the delightful way we were with Branagh and his interpretation of Brunel; moreover, it is beyond the organisers to invoke a series of Shakespearian characters; a Jane Austin heroine or one of Charles Dickens' various rogues. The reason for the presence of the children's literary villains is due to the presence of children acting as a centrepiece to the hospital-set segment, a short performance that depicts the enemies in giant puppet form rearing up and attempting to quash the children's apparent safety.

The segment as a whole was deceptive, in that it carried a message more broadly pertaining as to how Britain's best loved and most well-known institutions were capable of keeping the children of modern Britain safe when that could not have been any further from the truth. We must understand that this was at a time when the very ideology at the core of the ceremony, not to mention the entire sporting event, in the form of multiculturalism, had made it quite possibly the worst time in the country's history to be below the age of fifteen. The lax attitude maintained within both the institutions of the police force and social working sector throughout various cities around the United Kingdom made it possible for well organised prostitution rings specialising in under-aged girls to operate on a large scale and for many decades unperturbed.

Moreover, with the 2011 death of television personality Jimmy Savile, there erupted a series of revelations pertaining to Savile's own sexually-charged predatory behaviour whilst working with the institution of the British Broadcasting Corporation decade go. This was something which even extended towards the victimising of children at hospitals, an apparent safe haven according to the opening ceremony. What followed on from this was a series of disclosures relating to a number of BBC radio disc jockeys, whose own attitudes towards minors began to surface and whose actions and being able to get away with it for so long brought into question the integrity of another one of the United Kingdom's treasured institutions. It did not help that, not so long afterwards, even politicians were apparently susceptible to accusation when former Members of Parliament Cyril Smith; Greville Janner and Leon Brittan, some after their deaths, had the uncomfortable sensation of accusation hovering over their heads.

Having at least paid homage to the National Health Service, we reach the 1960's, and here begins a series of celebrations of aspects of culture at the lower end of its spectrum. Bubble-gum pop music is indispersed with more modern concepts of social networking, performances directed towards people in the audience both there in the stadium and at home observing on television – the likes of whom must have watched on in stunned bewilderment at the earlier performances of cricket matches; village green life and the presence of those distinctly spindly Middle Age-era flags adorning poles which might otherwise be used for jousting. The ceremony arrives at the 1990's, utilising various pop songs to prop up a makeshift narrative about a young, single woman who loses her cellular phone during a night out within which she was looking to win a date with a stranger so as to initiate a longer term relationship. Eventually, she is reunited with both of it *and* the young man who found it, in what is actually a somewhat charming episode which looks at love transcending generations and eras.

The centrepiece amidst the otherwise unrestrained chaos of the bouncing, bounding and colour-filled exhibitionism of various youths streaming through the decades of twentieth Century pop music arrived in the form of a rendition of *Abide With Me*. With the arena blacked out from beyond where the spotlights shone in the centre, one of the biggest reveals as to how the opening ceremony for *any* Olympic meeting exists for the spectacle of television arrives in the form of a young dancer from the sub-continent, who initiated his own otherwise totally alien to London and Britain dance routine to the pulsating thumping of drums recreating a steady heartbeat. In the midst of all of this stands Emeli Sande, someone charged with singing the iconic melody which would have sufficed all by itself as a standalone singing performance.

With multiculturalism, however, at the epicentre of both this spectacle individually and the wider Olympic project, there was thus created this strange manifestation of a song dating back generations, which the onlooker may or may not have even heard, featuring a black Scottish woman singing to the spectacle of an extraordinarily flexible dancing arrangement deriving from the sub-continent. Aside from the evident multicultural gentrification, what made the production number all the more disturbing was the manner in which a lighting prop was used to signify a rising sun; this small yellow orb being physically manoeuvred around at the start of the segment appearing almost to represent a literal dawning of a new era, an era whereby the black Scottish woman and the Asian dancer could occupy London and look to engage in something much more synonymous with a pre-revolutionary Britain.

Amidst the music, there was room for a surprising comedy sequence involving the incumbent Monarch and head of the Commonwealth, Queen Elizabeth the Second. For it was here that one of Britain's more renowned cultural exports in James Bond, played by then Bond-actor Daniel Craig, was transported to Buckingham Palace via the somewhat humble means of a black taxi cab in order to meet her. Wading through the corgi dogs and interior rooms draped in affluence and history, they exchange glances before retreating to a helicopter in order to venture across London to the stadium.

With a second helicopter to the television camera circling above the stadium, and teasing cuts from the floor inside the stadium to the interior of the helicopter supposedly housing both the Queen and James Bond, the unthinkable happened and a parachutist dressed in what the Queen was roughly wearing leapt from it. The punch-line was somewhat ruined when it became evident that the footage of Craig and the Queen in the helicopter *about* to jump was quite evidently taking place during some of the brighter parts of a day – the likes of which did not quite sync up with what it was that they were jumping out into; namely, the near-pitch black of well into the night.

While immensely surprising, it was ultimately a moment that invited people to laugh at a figure of authority – in many ways, the ultimate in such a thing: the head of the state themselves. In many ways, it was a moment more broadly attached to the way the police officer or the school teacher faced being held by a liberal-leaning stranglehold due to a culture of political correctness and institutional reform; something which removed their authority and stopped them from correcting those of a younger disposition with the hand of discipline when it was needed.

When the time came for the participating teams to emerge, the stagnation in what one could literally look at, in that proceedings now consisted of people merely filing out onto a running track, ran in perfect synchronisation with the two hours of unfolding political projection that was just witnessed. The reason for this was that it was at this point that we had to return to the concept of countries; flags and, via what it was that a number of people from several nations from the Middle East and South Pacific were wearing, national identity.

The energy and vibrancy of any opening ceremony is often lost when the time comes for something known as the "Parade of Nations" to occur. On the other hand, the cordial unveiling of the people actually participating might come as relief if the spectacle itself has been underwhelming or too long. This point in the show is, after all, where everything would have started in the first place were it not for the spectacle driven thirsts of television. But here, at London 2012, was a gargantuan leap; a jump from a celebration of diversity and Britain's journey from suspicious and otherwise quirky pasts very few in the auditorium could relate to, to certain people exhibiting national pride.

When the time came for the Great Britain team to emerge, it received the loudest cheer of the evening. The tension was palpable, the anticipation almost unbearable; the final few countries were so small in the number of athletes they sent, for instance the Virgin Islands and Yemen, that there was a distinct impatience for the announcer to get on with it and reach to the showstopper: the revealing of "Team GB". When they did finally enter the arena, they did so into the now pitch black night but for the stadium's incredibly powerful floodlights: behind the alphabetically last-placed Zimbabwe, whose few moments of being the centre of attention would not have merited the hours of waiting for it back stage.

The first half of their lap around the stadium and into the centre for the formalities was to the immensely inappropriate *Heroes*, by David Bowie; a song too wrapped up in that counter-culture era of 1960's rock-and-roll for it to be in any way suitable. Yet, it was the perfect fit for what was about to play out over these next fourteen days; made possible by people who, for some, would have seen this as their anthem.

What became more alarming, after a series of long shots doing well to capture the excitement and grandeur of the occasion, was the manner in which things descended into near farce when "Heroes" ended and *Galvanise*, by the Chemical Brothers, began. This particular piece, immensely inappropriate and rendering the occasion little more than an open-air disco, supported the spectacle of screeching young female athletes who had had the television camera thrust into their faces and saw them barely able to conceal their hysteria.

There was not a calm; rational and, you might say, quintessentially "British" reaction of excitement and fervour which may have been more measured and more conservative in the past. When the broadcast settled on some young black athletes, the music, a largely instrumental track which inflects distinctly Arabian chords into its overture around thumping drum and bass, which further still combines with rap, so thoroughly diverse, suddenly overlaid images of these particular athletes breaking into a relaxed pose more typically associated with an African American rap musician.

Watching on, an applauding David Cameron sat beside Deputy Prime Minister Nick Clegg; both of them enjoying the spectacle and in no way put off by a festival which he himself may not have had a hand in creating, but saw fit to laud when the time came. This gave way to the speeches from Sebastian Coe, speaking as head of the bid, and Jacques Rogge, head of the

International Olympic Committee at the time. What Coe had to say might just have well have been a modern, centrist politician attempting to talk up the concept of ethnic diversity within a London borough so as to win votes; with the sentiment that best captured what he meant *by* his speech being: "London 2012 will inspire a generation".

Precisely what Coe meant by this is unclear, for he did not back the remark up with a context. Inspire a generation to do what? Swim? Run? Drive taxis? Become lawyers? Emigrate? The short answer is that people were supposed to, having witnessed the Games, embrace multiculturalism in such a way so that no political party too far to the right of the centre ground would ever again come anywhere near winning an election. They were supposed to feel at ease living amongst Islam and not to feel ashamed at initiating a relationship with someone of a differing ethnicity. They were not supposed to feel ill-at-ease with a homosexual marrying another, nor even adopting children: an experiment which pushes society, indeed a civilisation, down rather radical and unheralded routes.

The unmentioned state answer is, at least according to their promotional bidding material, that it will induce sporting excellence and encourage people to take up recreational activity. To speak of an obesity problem, and that London 2012 was coined to tackle this as per Rogan & Rogan, would be to essentially admit there was a problem at all - something politicians have a tough time in doing. Meanwhile, Rogge reminded everyone that London was now the first city to host the Games three times. This came with the incorrect assertion that London was "...welcoming the world to this diverse, vibrant cosmopolitan city yet again" – an attempt at blinding people to the immense changes the city had undergone *since* 1948, and a somewhat fatuous attempt to draw parallels between the white, monocultural and properly governed Britain and London of the post-War years with the Hellish, pluralistic one of the twenty-first century.

Various dignitaries were then, as tradition demands, invited to carry the Olympic flag to the pole upon the green hill where the ceremony began so that it may fly. If the green mound was supposed to represent an England, indeed a Britain, of so long ago that it predated the industrial revolution, and that the Olympic flag itself is read into by some social critics as an epitome of internationalism and globalisation, its placement at the very top of said mound amongst the flags of the world in that small pocket of London was more than just apt. In amongst the personnel carrying the flag prior to this was a certain Doreen Lawrence, who, like Nelson Mandela without anyone actually thinking about it, has become a beacon of Leftist Utopian idolatry.

This is due to fact her son was murdered in 1993 by some white supremacists, despite the fact that lots of different people from all kinds of different racial and cultural backgrounds killed all the time in Britain by lots of other kinds, but also largely because the police investigation that followed this murder eventually revealed that they had been doing most of their investigating on the Lawrence family themselves. The consensus that this was "institutional racism" was reached very quickly; Lawrence's peerage in the House of Lords and consequent promotion to cultural icon (really just a Leftist pawn) representing diversity and tolerance has followed her around ever since.

Also present at the moment was American boxer Muhammad Ali, himself a figure of politics more broadly associated with anti-establishment philosophies and civil rights activism; a man who, despite winning a gold medal for the United States in 1960, returned home to racial segregation and a man who, during the Vietnam War, lost his right to practise boxing in the United States because of his refusal to have anything to do with said strand of American foreign policy.

Ali's lighting of the Olympic flame in 1996, in of all places the Georgian city of Atlanta located down there in the Deep South, neatly encapsulated as to how far the United States had, certainly in its own eyes, moved on with regards to reforming its attitudes towards a variety of things not limited to diversity and civil rights. In London, Ali's presence was superfluous in the grander scheme of the ceremony – he did not contribute to any great extent that might have seen the ceremony lose something had he not been there. But he was, like Lawrence and the strange preoccupation with Mandela during the build-up to the Games, vital to being there in the sense that he encapsulated what the designers of the Games wanted to promote philosophically.

What followed was the Olympic flame, something which we have already seen was coined by the Nazis upon some very unnerving foundations, being run around the Olympic arena by a set of diverse young athletes chosen further still by a set of diverse *former* athletes. This entire process is played out to a chorus of really rather eerie angelic music, courtesy of an ethnically diverse children's choir acting as the backdrop to a lone singer and accomplice, whose job it was to sound out individual notes on a large xylophone. The entire performance carried with it a very strange air of complete revisionism; a heavenly aesthetic, both visually and orally, of life beginning again as one chapter ended and another began, as if a life had ended and these are the gates of the afterlife to which you are now ascending.

Then came the seminal moment; the moment where it all fell into place: the actual lighting of the Olympic flame which would supposedly burn for the two week duration of the sporting spectacle. This was not fulfilled by anybody particularly famous, in spite of the teasing throughout the show that it may be one of David Beckham or Sir Steven Redgrave. Instead, and in true Leftist political thought, it was nobody with any great reputation or prestige who lit the flame, for it was each of the aforementioned young runners themselves who crouched down and lit some of small black objects that had been carried into the arena during the teams' entrances and tactfully placed. When the plan finally came to fruition, the small black objects rose to form one mighty post-modern cauldron made out of rods now harbouring the Olympic flame.

Like the Socialist Party of Great Britain, who list their candidates to the European Parliament alphabetically instead of by order of preference to avoid the concept of 'one' being better than 'another', everybody and nobody lit the flame.

We have already, albeit briefly, looked at how those who light the Olympic flame at the culmination of the Olympic Opening Ceremony carry with them a specific political significance. The act in itself has, over the years, become a central, seminal moment in the Olympic host nation's duties. Rarely are there ten or so seconds set aside, in any political walk of life, that act as a better opportunity to showcase to the world who you are and from what socio-political direction you are deriving than that of the ignition of the Olympic flame.

This ignition is often a very famous moment. From the day Adolf Hitler utilised such a thing to try and highlight his nation's strong ties to a glorious past of developed, forward thinking white Greek civilisations right the way up to Britain's own 2012 spectacle of inclusivity, various examples of dignitaries fulfilling such an act have come and gone over the decades. Along the way, as briefly explored already, this has been used by various nations and cities in order to make a statement; to put across who they are *now* and how they want to present that in the personnel utilised to fulfil the ignition. Hitler's embodiment of how it was Germany now had its roots in muscular, white ancient Greece in choosing Fritz Schilgen to light the flame set an absolute precedent in this regard, carrying on to Tokyo 1964 when a survivor of the August 1945 Hiroshima bomb lit the cauldron so as to state to the world that of Japan's re-emergence out of the mire.

Japan are involved again, albeit indirectly, with regards to the 1988 Games which took place in South Korea. The gentleman who carried the torch into the stadium during the opening ceremony, although technically did not play a part in *lighting* the flame, was a certain Sohn Kee-chung. Sohn was a Korean runner who was forcibly competing for the Japanese at the Berlin Games of 1936 due to Korea's being invaded *by* the Japanese. His wonderful achievement of winning a gold medal in the marathon that year thus only counted towards Japan's total, yet he was brave enough to break protocol and utilise the achievement to raise awareness on his nation's plight, while back in Korea, a newspaper had controversially published the photograph of him crossing the winning line with Japan's emblem on his tunic artificially removed in editing. As a result of this stepping out of line, the outlet was shut down by the now ruling Japanese and the staff imprisoned.

Thus, Sohn Kee-chung's selection to play a part in the Seoul festivities carried with it a cutting, socio-political dynamic in that it represented as to how free South Korea now was and Sohn epitomised not only sporting gravitas and ability but staunch bravery in the face of callous adversity. Muhammad Ali's in 1996, somewhat well-disguised as the rouse it was, then gives way to London's surrender to diversity in allowing seven separate youngsters, each aspiring athletes in the way Amber Charles was when she personally delivered the 2004 official bid, to light the flame and announce to the world that fourteen days of sporting competition had started.

While Hitler's was certainly the first, London's and, indirectly Blair's, will not be the last. It is difficult to predict as to in what form these subtle, often destructive, political manifestations might appear next. The Summer Olympics, spaced broadly in this sense across a four year cycle, thus only presents us with an instance of an Olympic flame being lit very periodically. The pool of nations capable of realistically fulfilling Olympic hosting duties is a relatively small one of developed North American and European first-world cities, the likes of which only sometimes gives way to intermittent ventures further afield to a venue bordering the Pacific.

Opportunities along the lines of what Britain had in 2012 to do what they did are scarce, for to find a locale wherein you could feasibly host an Olympics in the first place that underwent the bidding process correctly enough to win, and then only to utilise said sporting event to showcase to the world immense internal political change, is rare. The likelihood of actually finding an instance whereby the lighter of the Olympic flame, or one of the significant torchbearers, is meant to personify a political statement, or ideology prolonged by those either behind the bid or running the country, will always come second to a mere famous face or decorated sporting personality *from* that country.

This is not to say it cannot happen at all, for its roots in Berlin were built upon the foundation of this very idea; the retaining of the concept of the Olympic flame, despite its National Socialist roots, to be exhibited during the Olympic festivities actually allows for leaders and politicians to utilise a moment to advertise to the world a newfound sense of self, or indeed to rally a population around a thought process which might otherwise be harmful to a society. In London 2012 and Berlin 1936, we saw this in a very raw and deeply uncompromising way.

And so, we observe that the opening ceremony to the 2012 Summer Olympic Games in London had, in itself, numerous elements of political discourse and several politicised statements to make. Some were less obvious than others, whereas others were more striking, but all of it was bound together by the same tactical approach of delivering the message through performance and colour. While its politics were not subtle, the ceremony itself was. This may have been highly political, but it was not *overtly* political: there were no oversized Union Jacks being trooped along by marching hordes of those belonging to the British army as there might have been at a politically driven parade in the era of Berlin '36; no militaristic display akin to what the Soviet Union might have done in their day or North Korea now.

The opening ceremony was not a rally of any sorts, more synonymous with the marching hordes of soldiers gripping heroically to the nation's flag attributable to the hard left or hard right. Moreover, it was the celebration of something through discourse and argument; the kind of intellectual conquest those left of centre are more synonymous with in their hunger for Fabian invasion. The show began and ended with that same green mound which, once upon a time and many centuries ago, looked over an exhibition of humble farming; gentlemanly bat-and-ball games; cottages; streams and apparent normality and calmness. By the end, all of that is gone, although bits and pieces of it do still remain in fits and starts across the land. In its place, fittingly, the flags of practically every country in the world adorn various parts of that mound; carried up unopposed by a variety of racially and culturally diverse people, most of whom now essentially lay claim to it.

For all the discourse, indeed effort on behalf of the founding fathers of the modern Olympic movement, on keeping the Olympics for amateurs and a shining beacon for amateurism, there was certainly a fair share of professional and otherwise millionaire tennis players leading their teams out. There was often, in fact, giddy excitement from the commentators as another personality in the form of Maria Sharapova; Novak Djokovic or Marcos Baghdatis bore their respective nations' flags for Russia; Serbia and Cyprus. Otherwise, nondescript Austrian swimmers; Malaysian squash players; Romanian gymnasts and the like were greeted with the same hushed tones any person would grant them.

The ceremony itself focussed heavily on what happened both to and in Britain in the twentieth century, with, as stated, a perverse 'fast-forwarding' through some of the more memorable chapters in the United Kingdom's history which paused only to really encompass the industrial revolution and World War One. There was no real mention of London's prior hosting duties of 1908 and 1948, as if such things did not happen. We recall from an earlier chapter theories pertaining to how new orders like to bury their past, the likes of which they are ashamed and too fully focussed on the new era of whatever their discernible politic is to either care or pay homage. Recall as to how [16]"One of the most striking features of mega-events is how rarely they utilise the sites of previous events, almost as if they wanted to avoid taking on the ideological detritus of a former conjuncture" pertained to the demolition of White City Stadium and Wembley's twin towers, whereas the burying of the previous British Games in the opening ceremony was largely a desire to wipe a specific slate clean.

There was an incredibly awkward moment when the German team entered, with the camera cutting to an otherwise anonymous official who appeared to be providing the large squad, as they walked past him, a mock-Nazi salute. Perhaps, however, it was it was merely a gesture designed to acknowledge the otherwise quite addictive soundtrack accompanying all this: *Saturday Night Fever*, by the Bee Gees.

Otherwise, British Broadcasting Corporation commentator Barry Davies found it amusing that Iran and Iraq would enter the arena consecutively; a female Saudi Arabian competitor made the "v", for victory, sign with her index and middle fingers as she walked into the arena – perhaps signifying the Saudi regime's generally victorious status over the British elite and their economy. Or, contrarily, and given the young woman was unveiled and thus baring much of her upper body and face, illegal in Saudi Arabia for a woman, perhaps it was a statement, with its roots in western feminist philosophy, directed towards the Saudi patriarchy that she was here, in London, and free to do such a thing. Whatever the drive toward the signal, we observe how easily the essence of politics or a political statement finds its way into sporting spectacle.

The response to the whole thing was largely what one would expect from the liberal establishment, which begs the question therefore, if few are of the opinion that the establishment is worth anything, why did anyone think it was as worthwhile as *they* thought it was? David Cameron spoke in particularly glowing terms of it, believing it to have been [17]"a great showcase of this country" and later adding that it was...[18]"...a brilliant effort to bring it together, our past, our future and the vibrancy of the country...", thus completely confirming his commitment to state-multiculturalism and that he had so much more in common with the left than the right, although any expansion on what he thought of it in more detail is difficult to uncover.

Moreover, his response to Conservative Member of Parliament Aidan Burley is easier to find. Burley, himself fired from a senior position in the Conservative-led Coalition of 2010-15 just prior to the Games for attending a Nazi themed stag-party, described the ceremony as [19]"The most leftie opening ceremony I have ever seen - more than Beijing, the capital of a communist state!" and added, once the athlete's parade had begun, [20]"Now we can move on from leftie multi-cultural crap. Bring back red arrows, Shakespeare and the Stones!", although here failing to spot that the Rolling Stones, to which he alluded, were just as wrapped up in the politic of what he had just witnessed as anything else.

It was only later when Burley's apologies arrived, after he had borne the brunt of the Leftist reaction from various Labour Members of Parliament and prominent ex-footballer Stan Collymore. Even Cameron attacked this position, describing what he said as... [21]"...completely wrong, an idiotic thing to say." This was a project that was long in the making; something coined when Burley was a long way from the political heights he found himself occupying in 2012, and those responsible for it were quite evidently not prepared to allow someone to happen upon an opinion at the twelfth hour which might force sets of opinions into people's heads that it was anything short of faultless. Alas, it, like the Games it initiated, was a long way short of faultless.

If London's opening ceremony was a very precise and drawn out, although slickly executed, exhibition of colour; lights and pyrotechnics, the likes of which was often quite political, its closing ceremony was a punchier, sharper and more derivative spectacle. The fact it was not even anything remotely memorable, and largely consisted of absolutely nothing in particular for the first hour, before descending into the bright, irrelevant noise that it was; a shambles of a display which too often looked like it had been dipped in a vast vat of Roy Lichtenstein before laid out to dry, ought to be enough to suggest that it was performed almost begrudgingly.

It is, again, worth reminding people that closing ceremonies exist because television exists – the fancier and more cutting edge television screens become, and the more plentiful the ways of watching television come about, the more organisers are forced into stepping up just what it is people are even watching. This is often why every four or so years that these ceremonies occur, the latest becomes the best ever one, and is why the pushing of the envelope must happen at the rate that it does – viewing a lot of what constituted as opening ceremonies from years ago, indeed even reading descriptions of them from eras before television, has them appear basic and quite unspectacular. This is because they are ultimately superfluous, and are not events that could not consist of a series of handshakes and speeches - all of which might be executed within one hour.

Beginning in the early evening on what had been a warm, clear day in southern England, the Closing Ceremonial broadcast began with a brief outlining of artistic director Gavin Kim's visual hypothesis. Specifically, how the show would [22]"...be a celebration of all that is good about London; British people; British music and British culture." In addition to this, we are told, or perhaps warned, of [23]"...several different interpretations of the British flag". What this would eventually come to consist of was all of the messier, more reformist characteristics of the *opening* ceremony but louder and more informal; a celebration, more brash and physical in presentation because subtlety no longer mattered, of trashy; throwaway; pop, often sexualised, modernist bastions of British culture that had already been used as battering rams against the conservative ideas which had safeguarded the nation's identity for so long.

As was the case with the opening ceremony, there was a complete blank with regards to anything that happened before a certain point in the twentieth century; perhaps more so here, for people were not even given the chance to gawp quizzically at life in England of old but for the shower of colourful music and lights. Under the guise of celebrating the best of British, what has for a very long time come to represent a reformist anthem of sorts for the New Left, in John Lennon's *Imagine*, is broadcast to the audience. Large, spontaneous cheers greet this; cheers which perpetuate when grainy footage appears of Lennon himself singing it.

This actually rather blunt display in many ways topped anything that was ever put on in Berlin by Adolf Hitler; the Marxist chords of wishing for a world without nations; borders; ownership and religion fell rather easily, despite not having anything to do sport per se, into the sphere of what the Olympic Games of 2012 represented and was evidently on the minds of the organisers as worthy of a centrepiece. Indeed, behind the veil of acknowledging one of Britain's great song writers; politically outspoken figures and cultural icons lay something quite untoward, made nastier by the spectacle of a small pyramid of children as young as eight singing the song in the angelic manner they can only muster as the next generation is prepped.

Things move on to George Michael and *Freedom*, which of course neatly encapsulates the very free and easy philosophies the minds behind the games grew up with decades ago and epitomised how both liberally minded and inclusive London was supposed to be in modern times. Meanwhile, the decision to cut to a shot of the Union Jack turning bright pink on the floor of the venue from many hundreds of feet above the stadium should strike us as one of the instances mentioned earlier about Britishness being reconstructed, or "interpreted", to mean something else. This occurs shortly after what is, in retrospect, a quite bizarre segment celebrating famous British models; something which encompasses several black and white photographs of billboard size being tugged around the arena on trailers. The celebration, done so again under the guise of feeling proud that we have produced so many famous models, is actually one of sex and sex appeal; one of throwaway pop culture and modernistic materialism. The performance quite literally concludes with an unveiling of several of Britain's top models - one of whom is Georgia May Jagger, daughter of Mick Jagger, who in many ways epitomised the whole aesthetic of this segment with his dangerous music and 'look' in the 1960's.

The musical performances continue with relatively innocuous displays from Ed Sheeran; Liam Gallagher and Muse, items of which would not be so out of place at any popular music concert, but a handful of others catch the eye for reasons entirely linked to the reasons the Olympics were what they were from a British perspective and why it was that either ceremonies were as they were. One of which is popular comedian Russell Brand's version of *I am the Walrus*, a rendition which ultimately placed a low emphasis on vocals and a high one on spectacle for a very astute reason; a performance which, in many ways, encompassed everything wrong with a lot of liberal modernism in its pseudo-psychedelic venturing down a lane of *Beatles* nostalgia accompanied by an array of oddly dressed male performers and some scantily dressed female ones.

There was nothing "British" about Brand's performance, for it was a performance that could not be categorised as distinct to any 'nation'. This was due to its content, which was, like so much of leftist liberal thinking, frilly; colourful and with a fancy looking surface but ultimately hollow and insubstantial with a view to being quite damaging. The same might be said of Fat Boy Slim's turn on the London stage, a rendition of one of his more popular pieces taking place to the backdrop of, of all things, a giant inflatable octopus and a few dozen young dancers complimenting that of an aesthetic more akin to an indoor rave. The performances by singers Jessie J and Tinie Tempah, meanwhile, inflected an element of the African-American rap scene to proceedings, what with their respective appearances in the attire that they wear and the vehicles with which they utilise to navigate the stage.

Perhaps the best instance of a performance, from either of the opening and closing ceremonies, encapsulating what the London Olympics was and what said ceremonies desperately tried to represent was that of Eric Idle's rendition of *Always Look on the Bright Side of Life*. The culturally aware among those who saw the ceremony, or who are even reading this now, will instantaneously spot a connection to the immensely divisive 1979 film *A Life of Brian*; a film which is largely regarded as to having had a damaging and quite deliberately irreversible effect on the United Kingdom as a predominantly Christian country. The Olympic edition rekindles what could feasibly be described as a 'tradition' in this regard, with its depiction of angels as being these heavenly and rather sexually glamorous women, as an array of nuns dance around to the chaos of Idle leading proceedings – periodically lifting the lower part of their tunics to reveal pantaloons in the design of the Union Jack. In any case, the target is Christianity, and far from being a bit of fun and an homage to something British that was famous and is now worth celebrating in the here and now, it was, like the choral odes to Lennon and reluctance to speak out against both R&B music and personalities playing a large part in forging our youth's identities, an embracing of everything these things represented and a desire to want to pursue them further.

Pop group The Spice Girls were, wittingly or otherwise, entirely wrapped up in the liberal push to the left which best encapsulated the London Olympics. On 6 October 2001, there aired a BBC television programme entitled *I Love 1996*; an otherwise quite baffling one off show which documented a time not long ago enough for its viewers to feel in any way nostalgic about its content, and furthermore mostly depicting interviews with the people involved that were still young enough to be doing what the show was about. The show largely depicts the liberalism that had already infiltrated most of Britain's institutions, the likes of which eventually gave way to the landslide that was the 1997 General Election. This is best represented in the revelling of the drama *This Life*, which chose to depict all manner of seedy and sexually deviant behaviour in its telling of the story of men and women in their twenties living together in London.

Enter the reassessment of The Spice Girls during said retrospective on the year before Year Zero, whose colourful attire and the pumping confidence of its members lights up the sofas of most talk shows as they attempt to sell to the viewer the philosophy of "Girl Power" totally unfazed by the authority of the presenter and demonstrating no desire to display any kind of restraint at being on television. The video to their 1996 debut track *Wannabe*, depicting the girls smashing through a stately home and upsetting the present hierarchy, is looked upon by the programme as synonymous with the trend at the time of obliterating established norms with a sweeping blow of fresh, youthful new order.

The girls themselves, in many respects, epitomise a strand of diversity which we would not necessarily see as predominant in the public eye until the Games themselves. They break down both class and racial prejudices with their lone black member contrasting four white women, one of whom, Emma, possesses an Aryan-like physical appearance; furthermore, they make a concise distinction between certain "posh" members (whose husbands later played their own part in securing the Games) and your more regular, down to earth sport-loving working class members, who wear football shirts and derive from Liverpool. This is all propped up by a fifth member made distinguishable by their ginger hair.

When the time came for BBC Three to air *Olympics 2012: 50 Greatest Moments* later that year, a contributor made reference to how what is now known as "Super Saturday", when several of Britain's athletes won almost as many gold medals, epitomised the success of Britain's diversity. This lay with the fact that not only did Ennis and Farah each win gold medals, but even long jumper Greg Rutherford did too – this, the contributor asserted, was worthy of inclusion for Rutherford's hair was ginger. While meant only semi-seriously, it manages to find a way to tie in with the above with regards to how The Spice Girls suddenly became relevant enough again to perform at London's closing ceremony.

The closing ceremony was essentially confirmation that London 2012 had nothing left to give, for there was nothing really left to do but sit back and observe the legacy – the likes of which would take years to materialise anyway. The idea had been hatched a decade earlier; kicked around by a very specific set of reformist politicians who did not think they had much of a chance in fulfilling what they wanted to do, but who grew in confidence when the bid management changed in 2004 and their attempt reached the finals stage. Once these advances had happened, the London team began to play their hand a little more; the inclusivity of the city and the people running it became more apparent – young black girls, in the form of Amber Charles, were used to figurehead the project's core philosophy, while the background aesthetic of the bid generally was one of diversity and reform: a reshaping of London and the use of what was worth celebrating about London the most in using a few dozen young children of varying backgrounds and ethnicities.

This all gave way to the Games themselves, where the right people stepped into the right roles and, like actors in a stage play, manoeuvred their way around the world's most luxurious sporting stage fulfilling their parts: Jessica Ennis was the poster-child, the newfound beacon that Coe had essentially spent the last eight years dreaming of forging for the next generation. Mohamed Farah was the plastic Briton brought in to desensitise Islam, his role as double champion used to help extinguish the horrible memories of the day after London won the bid, when Muslims were responsible for blowing a little part of the city up. Lutalo Muhammad was the inclusive selection over the actual world champion in his discipline, the more mundanely named Aaron Cook. The male gymnastics team ended up on the podium after a disqualification above them, while Nicola Adams boxed her way to gold and glory – either sets of personnel fulfilling their roles as subverts of traditional gender driven roles.

There was very little left to either give or say when the closing ceremony came around, merely to rub salt into the wounds of those who did not agree with what the Olympics represented and perform some songs. The exhibition itself, more a series of live action music videos, was representative of a project that had concluded having been a rousing success – people had tuned in via the television; attended events and disciplines in their droves and had generally bought in to the Olympic sub-culture of two weeks long. In many ways, an actual *closing* ceremony was unwanted – the powers that be had not thought forward this far because there was no need. The first thought that comes to mind upon winning the rights to any event is not as to how the closing ceremony might look and London's glib, vacuous and ultimately low-culture dominated display was symptomatic of both this as well as the fact the London 2012 train had completely run out of fuel.

There was nothing left to do; nothing left to give. All that remained was to dig up a few famous names and faces from times past to rub the noses of those who might disagree with much of what London offered in the proverbial. This encompassed a diverse array of talent ranging from The Spice Girls to the master of much of what was imbued into the core of the 2012 Summer Olympics in Eric Idle himself. Along the way, an extraordinary amount of musical performance from many-a band and personality very much suggested that the show was geared towards the younger eye and mind, for they were ultimately for whom the Games were created and were expected to be the ones who took away from them the most.

CONCLUSION:
LAYING THE FOUNDATION FOR THE FUTURE

Track and field will always be the purest form of sport. An event which falls within the confines of it might, in its simplest form, consist of picking something up and whosoever can throw it furthest wins; the first one to the finish line a hundred meters away comes away with the adulation; whosoever can jump the farthest is the champion. There are no catches or gimmicks. It is without regulations and complications: there is no leg before wicket rule; no convoluted 'en-passant' manoeuvre as there is on the chess board; no set of dense regulations for the lie of a golf ball.

But, at the London Olympic stadium and its surrounding venues for two weeks in 2012, it was the purest; simplest and most honest of sporting exercises played out in the most artificial of ways. People ran; leapt and threw. They swam and hurled themselves off boards into water; rowed and lifted weights. They used their well-chalked palms to keep a grip of spindly wooden apparatus and timed their shotgun blasts so as to shatter the airborne disc at precisely the right time.

But, the real show lay not in what was being achieved by the athletes but by the people responsible for putting them there in the first place; it lay not in who they were but often *what* they were.

This was evident through a variety of things, but the beginnings of trying to understand how this came to be at all lies in the accepting that many of Britain's institutions, and several of the sorts of roles synonymous with occupying public office, had already by the year 2000 been filled up with reformists; liberals and cultural revolutionaries whose political views originated from that period in their lives growing up in the afterglow of a lot of what Roy Jenkins was responsible for in the 1960's. This was the same for those occupying places in the United Kingdom's sporting circles and applied to those behind Britain's Olympic bid, from those at the forefront of such a thing to those writing the official account away from the frontline of the hard work.

One must understand that the project itself was the work of a coalition of a very specific Left leaning generation of individuals who sought to further their philosophy through the duress of sport behind the smokescreen of former athletes which happened to include Sebastian Coe. From promotional material pre-bid to the Closing Ceremony by way of the athletes charged with winning gold medals, London 2012 was, in every sense, the Olympic Games societal reformers who were young adults in the 1970's could only dream of putting on.

During the course of this work, we have looked at how the Olympics has the massive potential to move opinion; change public attitude and break into societies subtle, propagandistic ideas about how one could and should live. Berlin 1936 was the beginning of this within a modern context, while the twentieth century is littered with minute instances of politics interfering with what should otherwise be a harmless two week display of solidarity through sport. Often, we have seen how it can spill out into the likes of rugby, with regards to the 1995 World Cup. In February 2015, New Zealand shared the Cricket World Cup with Australia, but made a point to stage the opening game of the tournament in Christchurch because of its proximity to the fourth anniversary of a horrific earthquake there. Specifically, it was announce to the world as to how they had fought their way out of the set-back and successfully rebuilt.

With Hitler, the idea was always to demonstrate the superiority of the Aryan race through sporting prowess via the Games – both summer and winter. This was always in spite of demonstrating very little interest in the Games themselves; indeed, Germany had been awarded the rights to host them in 1931 – two years before Hitler's 1933 ascension to power. Stuck in a situation whereby his country had a little under three years to prepare for the world descending on his nation for a sports festival, Hitler had to react. Sceptical to them at first, it would later dawn on him through his advisors that they may be able to work in favour of the National Socialist cause.

Considering this, one questions as to whether he would have had anything to do with them were he to have come to power prior to the International Olympic Committee's awarding them to Berlin. Hilton points out that [1]"At first he had shown no interest in the Games, dismissing them as 'an invention of the Jews and Freemasons' and describing them as some sort of Judaistic theatre 'which cannot possibly be put on in a Reich ruled by National Socialists.'" This was, of course, before it occurred to him the enormous potential they had in demonstrating to the world Germany's newfound status as a superpower who had cast off the shackles of institutionalised Jewry and the Versailles treaty, and were once again strong.

Both Tony Blair and Ken Livingstone leapt at the chance to engage in the Olympic idea when they discovered that such a thing was heading their way. While once part of a political party who, in 1993, possessed local councillors who retracted in disgust at the idea of hosting an Olympics, both men were near enough the top of an organisation that could not only look past the enormous cost, but view it as an opportunity to demonstrate a specific politic. In spite of the fact he had [2]"...never been an avid sports fan..." we are informed by Lee, "...Livingstone got emotionally involved in the bid because of its potential to change the face of the place he loved."

The opportunity was of course too good to turn down – with a decade-plus of devolution already provided to the city of London through the devolution acts of the late-1990's, something which eventually led to the forming of a London Assembly and an elected mayor, Livingstone realised that there was a chance to move the capital of England on from its reputation as a stuffy white monocultural locality by way of the Games. In sync with Hitler and Berlin, a faithful servant, and individual those at the top knew to be on the same political wavelength as they were, was hired to play an important role in ferrying the Olympics into port so that it would resemble what those in charge wanted it to look like. This was Hans von Tschammer und Osten, Hitler's own Ken Livingstone in this instance, who was [3]"... appointed as Director of German Sports." He is described by Hilton as having been "...a loyal supporter [of the Nazis] since the early 1920s" but "...knew nothing about sport. His conduct as well as his ignorance should have disqualified him."

For the task of winning the 2005 bid, the team hired American Barbara Cassani; a business women without a sporting background, but nonetheless the right person to mobilise a disparate squad of writers; former athletes and political activists. Either her appointment was down to the fact she was the best for the job, and was thus an example of Labour betraying their policy on ignoring the best and brightest in favour of inclusive selection, *or* she was a living instance of Labour's desire to go beyond the traditional pale in hiring a minority for an important role so as to prove to the bigots of the world that such a thing can happen and happen successfully. In this case, the member of the group cut adrift from the traditionally 'male and pale' stock was a woman. Regardless, she could not do the job to the level she thought satisfactory and resigned within a year.

Blair, Livingstone and the rest of their team, of course, had no interest in Aryan supremacy like Hitler did in 1936. What was at the core of their political mantra, the likes of which have held the British population in such thrall that all of the mainstream political parties of this era have had to embrace in one way or another, was pluralistic multicultural inclusive diversity; a modern ideology forged the morning after the night before, when contemporary revolutionaries already drunk on a set of 60's reforms, which ranged from the contraceptive pill to the advent of television to the ridding of the death penalty and the decriminalisation of homosexuality, did what they did when they had the chance.

The Games itself, when the time came, were ultimately spearheaded by Jessica Ennis; a young woman from Labour heartland, whatever that meant by 2012; a product of a mixed race marriage and who would later come to be part of one herself – a living embodiment of a post-War Britain made stronger and more muscular, epitomised in Ennis' physique and sporting ability, by its inclusivity and immigration; someone who was much more than a mere athlete.

This was only really spotted by people after the Games themselves had happened, when Yasmin Alibhai-Brown pointed out as to how Ennis [4]"...symbolised the nation's altered DNA – a quiet, irreversible genetic revolution" in an *Independent* article in December 2012. With Sebastian Coe's child-orientated ideology at the core of the bidding process, twinned with the manner in which Ennis' rise to the peak of heptathlon, a deadly cocktail was forming whereby everything New Labour and their supporters stood for could be purveyed on the international stage alongside Coe's passionate desire to get children running; jumping and generally more athletic. Ennis' crossing of the line in that final heptathlon event, arms aloft – in full knowledge she was the champion, was essentially the cultural and political explosion everything had been building to.

Along a similar train, Mohamed Farah played a sort of second fiddle to Ennis; the two coming to forge a kind of unspoken double act of revisionist multiracialism that had been bestowed upon a country already in a spin as to what it was even supposed to be anymore. Born in Somalia and with most of his time spent training abroad in the United States, his role was ultimately to present to a watching audience a version of Islam that was embraceable and moderate. His successes on the track in the London Games came to represent pluralistic Britain's retort to a politic of hatred and malevolence which had actually taken place several years earlier on 7 July 2005, when a very different genre of Islam destroyed pockets of a city still dizzy from the news that multicultural London would be granted the opportunity to show off to the world just how diverse they really were.

Being an immigrant and representing more broadly, through where is based himself and where he was born, internationalist neo-liberalism, furthermore during a sporting event set up to encapsulate these very things in the first place by its French founder, he was representative of what good immigration could bring and why we were supposed to be stronger because of it. In London 2012's terms, it meant two more gold medals which otherwise would have gone to Somalia, who still would have languished near the bottom of the table anyway, but since he was running for Great Britain, our total saw us in the inverse situation of being the one's propped up by that of the nations below. This was, and still is, in many ways representative of Britain's neo-liberal inclined position as one of the world's leading economies, wherein the citizenry of the globe are asked to prop up multinational corporations and other institutions within the locale of London anyway.

On a more grounded level, and with Coe's ideology of bringing children into the fray as a result of the London Games, Farah's role was to promote a moderate Islam; to sanitise it within the popular eye and bring it into a sphere of thinking and acknowledgement in ways that local imams and various Muslims occupying top journalistic jobs had either refused or failed to do. The publishing of *Where's Mo?*, a puzzle book for children in the mould of *Where's Wally?,* shortly after the Games meant that infants throughout the breadth of the country were able to spend their spare time growing up hunting for a Muslim runner on a colourful page of activity.

Like a lot of what New Labour practised, the likes of which were bestowed upon a population and then only later labelled as being what it was, the 2012 Olympic project caught a lot of Labour members and liberal commentators (such as Alibhai-Brown) out in just how radical it really was. There was little talk between 2005 and the night of the opening ceremony of how the Games themselves might unfold, or what they might consist of within a racially political circumference when the time came for teams to be picked; ceremonies to be planned and athletes apart of the project to be pushed into the public eye during the buildup. The public and sports writing intelligentsia already had their heroes from Beijing from four years earlier, in Chris Hoy and Rebecca Adlington, to hone in on for when the time came, while the prospect of a British football team consisting of David Beckham and maybe led by Sir Alex Ferguson was as exciting as the potential there was at seeing Andy Murray competing at Wimbledon for the tennis gold.

After the Games, however, it really began to become clear as to just how viciously political the whole fortnight really was – the ceremonies were exciting and full of colour, but were puzzled as to how to deal with anything British from before the Windrush; the tendency to focus on male gymnasts and female boxers in the television coverage worked surprisingly well, and fitted in nicely with the politics which brought the Games to Britain in the first place; athletes such as Ennis and Farah, their status' as women; immigrants; Muslims; blacks; half-castes and involved in mixed race relationships, seemed to rise to the surface in the way it always seemed like they were supposed to when the time came – almost as if the entire thing had been pre-scripted, rehearsed and then executed.

Labour politicians not savvy to the project, either because they needed not initially know or were too far removed from the project to begin with, such was its distance in the past from their present situation, jumped at the fact the Games had ended up being what they were: detached from a Britain of old; not puritan and wholeheartedly anti-Conservative. During a *Question Time*, the flagship British Broadcasting Corporation debate show, broadcast in early 2014, Labour Member of Parliament Rushanara Ali was answering a question on immigration and reminded everyone that...

> 5"*As the daughter of someone who came here in the 1960s (during the) labour shortage, I recognise the positive contribution people make to our country and the strength in our diversity and we saw that in the 2020* [sic] *Olympics, the best show on Earth, and we thrived in our diversity.*"

Labour shortages are temporary, but immigration is of course permanent; the legacy, of which, are politicians such as Rushanara Ali. Her use of the word "diversity" within the context of the reply and question was revealing; the concept of being a nation made up of lots of other, smaller nations, and that that is what makes us better, perfectly in sync with the Olympic ideals of 2012.

One writer, in the form of Ben Carrington, seemed to pick up on what was radiating from the Fabian driven Olympic team as the Games neared. While actually cited in Horne & Whannel, Carrington demonstrates an awareness of the racism of the older sporting spectacles which the British Empire set up; of Britain's monocultural, mono-racial British past and finally how London 2012 had the potential to move ideas and attitudes away from one thing and into an irreversible other. It was his in 2010 book *Race, Sport and Politics* wherein he revealed this. He informs us that...[6]"...analysis of sport 'in an age still marked by the historical scars of empire and racial exclusion' remains an essential task" and goes on, we are told, to consider the [7]*"'importance of sporting spectacles' in shaping national identities."* We are then informed that Carrington [8]"...suggests that the London Olympics in 2012 may provide 'an important public space within which to re-imagine the national story'. The 2012 Olympics 'might just signal the revival of a truly multicultural nation finally at ease with itself'

All of this could have been foreseen, but predicting the exact way in which it would have all unfolded would have been almost impossible. Mike Lee, himself from a mining background and a convert to New Labour, had a book published as early as 2006 when the time came to depict the challenges and events surrounding winning the bid for 2012. The publisher, which was *Virgin*, lists the book's genre as falling within the category of "sport", with which there ought to be no questions, but also "current affairs". Thus, the socio-political tract is teasingly referred to and just generally put across that this book *does* indeed document a story which had a greater political significance to those who were involved in it and charged with having to experience it. In amongst these details were the philosophies, the likes of which were not shy in pertaining to political beliefs that leaned towards diversity; pluralism and multiracial multiculturalism.

Sometimes they were very physical, insomuch black teenager Amber Charles would be the one to physically "deliver" the bidding book to the International Olympic Committee; Coe and Blair would make a point to be photographed outside Downing Street for the cover, behind them a range of children from minority backgrounds, and dialogue on *Magic of London*, the short film used during the bidding presentation which would sell London as a post-revolutionary multicultural haven for absolutely anybody.

Other times, they were less physical and really mere admittances of what was going on. During Athens 2004, a story is recounted about those who would be picking the 2012 host the following year being allowed to attend British functions deliberately decked out so as to remind the delegates of Britain's moving away from an older image. Meanwhile, and upon hearing the news that London had passed the first round of voting whereby a number of inferior bids were discarded and the final list was settled on, renowned actor Ian McKellen is depicted thus: [9]"'This is the greatest city in the world!' Exclaimed McKellen... 'It has always welcomed outsiders, immigrants, visitors. The heart of London is beating faster with the great news we are on the short list – and about time too.'

Here, as with Ali, we observe an immediate jumping to the concepts of immigration and "outsiders"; as if there was some sort of connection between what was going on within the confines of the hearts and minds of the people trying to bring an otherwise disconnected sporting festival to a certain city and the practise of immigration. The connections are too evident; McKellen may have been enthusing about the fact that, when an Olympic Games happens, the world's media; athletes and fans alike descend on your nation for two weeks of sporting pursuit, but Lee felt duty bound to include it in the official book depicting how Britain came to obtain London 2012 in the first place.

Three years after the Games had finished, a debate in the House of Commons about the Games' legacy saw participants mask what was at the very core of the Games with regards to legacy by deflecting the discussion towards fiscal ramifications and obesity levels among the youth. There was, however, one remark from a Conservative Member of the House which cut to the heart of what had gone on for those two weeks in 2012 when they remarked that London 2012 had been [10]"...the very first "legacy games", with the legacy...built in from the outset. It challenged an outdated, crusty image of a faded Britain." Casting our minds back to events in Athens, as depicted by Lee, when a Greek villa was rented and the International Olympic Committee members were wooed with promises on what New Labour's Great Britain now epitomised, we observe some cross-party unity in the idea that 2012 challenged the idea of an older Britain defined by a very different makeup.

The inclusivity and the attitudes that best define the modern Olympic movement, that is to say from the era of after the Second World War, are best epitomised in the fact that by 1972, all three of the predominant axis countries of The Second World War had hosted the Olympic Games, while the likes of France; Britain and the United States (bar London's miraculous hosting in 1948) went without until at least 1984, with France as of 2020 yet to host the Games.

As we have already meekly observed, the ethic of the Olympic Games' movement after the War, defined as "Olympism" in attempting to unify everyone in a peaceful and tolerant state of mind through quasi-ideology, stepped in as a sort of global police force representative of coming together; forcing people to place differences aside and then having them put up with one another for a designated period of time through the funnel of sport. This was predominantly down to the organisation's own internal guilt, brought about by the having to live with the fact its then president Pierre de-Coubertin spoke warmly, albeit via recording, during Berlin 1936's opening ceremony with regards to what Hitler had achieved in Germany up to that point.

This is more broadly represented in a physical sense in the Olympic Charter, the likes of which underwent somewhat of an overhaul in 2004 so as to encompass rather radical views on acceptance; tolerance and equality, when all the organisation responsible is supposed to do is ferry around one of the most logistically complicated events in the world. It is, certainly on the basis of the various vote rigging scandals of the 1990's, perhaps too rich to accept lectures in gentlemanliness and good manners from an organisation whom, until quite recently, could not even get its own house in order and indeed even self-proclaim to have derived from a classist; sexist nineteenth century institution.

Lee exposes the inconvenient truths to the bidding procedures of the International Olympic Committee during the later passages of his book, by which time the

Singapore bidding decision is in its death throes, in that people officiating in choosing London over Paris were often swayed by last minute compliments and gifts; even going so far as to select which city, over everything else, they would perhaps enjoy spending time in with their spouses. Indeed, it is widely acknowledged that the situation which arose over the decision to choose Atlanta as hosts for 1996 carried with it the depressing air of fiscal reasoning when those making the demands over the television rights and mass-sponsorships had too large-a say in whether said American city should be chosen over the Greek city of Athens, who were hoping to host the games on the one hundredth anniversary of the first modern edition.

The Olympic charter itself mostly consists of common sense, particularly the verses on how being sporting and refraining from cheating are encouraged, for the Olympics are, ultimately, merely a very expensive sports day. To gentrify the routine action of partaking in a sport with the cavernous depths of subjects such as philosophy or politics seems unnecessary and, if anything, complicates what is otherwise a somewhat simplistic attitude and set of morals which either come naturally to a person or can be taught from an early age using patterns of teaching that borrow from stiff conservative (even Christian) values.

Taking one of the rulings from this reformed 2004 charter, we find the following: [11]"Any form of discrimination with regard to a country or person on grounds of race, religion, politics, gender or otherwise is incompatible with belonging to the Olympic Movement.". No one could realistically argue with this, in the sense that it preaches decency and respect, but burrowed somewhere within this is the blunt anti-discriminatory philosophy of the modern British Left, where conversation and constructive criticism, even allergy, to one or many of the harsh reforms applied to where one lives is instantly dismissed as bigotry or fascism.

The International Olympic Committee are, in actuality, surprisingly shy in enforcing the core of their own code – to many people's frustration, Russia were not stripped of hosting rights to the 2014 Winter Games for their then-recent restrictions on how homosexuals may live, while the likes of Saudi Arabia continue to be a part of the Olympic movement in spite of their own attitudes towards those they consider out of sync with the quintessentially Saudi way of life. There additionally came no evidence of a desire to take action on Uganda, whose 2014 governmental bill to formally illegalise homosexuality was roundly criticised by many for the brief period it was implemented.

It is noted that [12]"The goal of Olympism is to place everywhere sport at the service of the harmonious development of man, with a view to encourage the establishment of a peaceful society" which is fittingly what the domestic Left wing of many Western European nations, particularly Great Britain, have since signed up to bestowing upon its citizens whom routinely vote the parties spearheading this change back into power anyway. Most European societies, particularly Britain's, were already peaceful until a series of damaging reforms ranging from the complete overhauling of the policing and educational institutions that resulted in youngsters running riot on poorly policed streets to the very eager bestowing of Islamism upon various towns and cities which had never previously seen the like.

There is a somewhat clear desire by the liberal leaning British left to an organisation such as the Olympic Committee to further their politics of reform, something which is able to help provide the means to demonstrate the positives of tolerance and the ills of questioning why something very bad is happening either to you or near to you.

The International Olympic Committee have, in this sense, become the benevolent headmasters of faux world peace; flitting from place to place, contemporary lecture in hand, ordering the people daft enough to want the Games in the first place to adhere to a code of conduct or risk expulsion and humiliation. One can only image both the foot-tapping and the finger-drumming the Londoners of 1948 that would have accompanied a witless bureaucrat whittling on about peace and tolerance to a nation who had just successfully soaked up everything the Nazi war machine had thrown at them. "Who..." they would say "...is this organisation, fronted by a man we do not know, to demand that we adhere to these regulations of decency and common-sense in a nation that is not (and so far, has never been) responsible for any sort of ethic debauchery?"

The fact we needed Jacques Rogge standing there during the opening ceremony of London 2012 and reminding us how to get along with one another is a testament as to how far Britain, as a nation, has fallen behind; indeed, the world as a whole, for proper conservative attitudes, the likes of which defied the country for so long, have been all but eroded for multiple faith and multiple culture driven equality. So enthusiastically are we in welcoming in the third world, and so dismissive and full of scorn are we for times past, that we bring ourselves down to the level of those coming to us and must learn all over again. Here, we witness the contemporary Left's kinsmanship with an organisation such as the International Olympic Committee; the likes of which seek to spread a form of diversity and in 2012 were allowed to do so in a place that has all but fallen to a form of diversity brought about by a political organisation spearheaded by those such as Blair; Livingstone and Jowell.

If, in the eyes of two sports scientists, [13]"Sport in Britain has always been about far more than what actually happens on the field of play", then the London Games very much fell into this canon of thinking, and speaking out about it is both vital and necessary. It may feel fruitless warning, or speaking, of a lot of the content found within this work given the time that has elapsed since the Games, but let it be known that nothing anybody might have said or done prior the Games would have changed its nature, merely made people aware earlier. But, with the socio-political situation being what it is, what with the multiculturalism still rampant; the Islamification process flourishing and aggressive neo-liberalist economic policies being propped up by both the cheap labour mass immigration brings and the construction of iconic glass buildings solely so as to be sold off to the highest Gulf State bidder, and with the ten year anniversary of London winning the Games having arrived in July of 2015, both a post-mortem and a pointing out of the nature of the Games felt necessary.

Let it be known that this work was never meant to be a personal attack on the likes Jessica Ennis; Mohamed Farah or Tom Daley, or indeed anyone else competing at the Games whom I may have mentioned. These are people who trained hard and competed at what is considered the highest level within their chosen sporting disciplines in a dedicated and honourable fashion. I possess no affiliation to them; fondness *for* them and do not have a problem *with* them as people – only with how they were ultimately exploited as pawns in a broader game by the people with whom issues should lie. Reading *Unbelievable: From my Childhood Dreams to Winning Olympic Gold* by Jessica Ennis, an account of the author's various performances in an array of track and field tournaments and incorrectly described by many as an autobiography, it is evident that the time; energy; pain; effort and sacrifice required to partake at these things is like nothing I could have guessed without reading it.

However, behind all the fluffy disfigured mascots and away from the funny poses from star athletes, the 2012 Olympics was not the fun; innocent and entirely harmless spectacle of sports and entertainment that seem to come around every so often in various places throughout the world. Coe's assertion, the one responsible for opening this very work, during the closing ceremony of the Games, that "The spirit of these games will inspire a generation. When our time came, Britain, we did it right" was a lot more than a mere verbal patting on the back for the hundreds of volunteers whom helped bring the Games to life. It was a promise; a promise that the essence of diversity and liberal reform was not going anywhere in the foreseeable future and thus more-so resembled an act of political self-gratification that those who spearheaded it had done their jobs and done them well.

These were viciously liberal ideas based on the concept of a country being a home for anybody; where multiple ethnicities and their cultures could flourish, where mixed race relationships would not be seen as against mainstream type; where people were unified in spite of their class and where those who were otherwise ideological opponents, in Muslims and homosexuals, could share a designated space and a common flag. The political hydrogen bomb that was the 2012 Olympics, witnessed by all and observed around the globe, landed with such ferocity and preordained accuracy in its near complete destruction of everything that preceded it in British sporting tradition that its imprints are visible all over the country.

They are, in fact, as far reaching as the quiet, backwater territories of the south coast of England, past sleepy Winchester and within sight of the Isle of Wight, where there stands a basketball court hybridised with an asphalt football pitch complete with small recreational zone enabling your more typical playground activities. Adorning the entire zone are giant incarnations of the faces of the games drawn onto a brick wall, their Christian names written in sly "*London 2012*" italics just to the side of their image, which gaze indomitably down onto the space. "*Jessica*" it reads, in honour of the Games' epitome of Britain's ethnic pluralism. "*Mo*" it says again somewhere else, stopping short of course of using his full name: Mohamed.

We have encountered this political idolatry in the past, as these beacons of political ideology, the likes of which gave birth to your nation and are worthy of your adornment due to their being figureheads of your nation's founding ideology, adorn the towns and streets of one's home. In the case of London and Great Britain, the ideology was multiracial multiculturalism, but in the past has seen statues of Saddam Hussein stand tall in the centre of the Iraqi capital of Baghdad; Vladimir Lenin adorning town squares in the old Soviet Union and Karl Marx in Berlin. Murals in North Korea are often designed in such a way so as to give praise to that nation's founding father and his descendants.

The politically driven and incredibly imperialistic presence of these recreational arenas, part of London's legacy to enthuse children in sports and gym activity generally, are a permanent reminder of who is great and of what you are. It is a constant reminder of the revolutionary methods, more-so people, behind the practise because a statue of Sebastian Coe or Tony Blair would immediately give the game away. I hope that, within these pages, I expanded on the notion that the Olympics of the year two thousand and twelve was a somewhat sordid, twisted and ultimately vacuous political project to the extent that I wanted to; that it was the result of what happens when the politics of a movement like New Labour spills over into sporting spectacle, and that I put across the notion that said Olympics were a quite disturbing occasion where a nation was tricked into backing a celebration of Britain that had nothing to do with Britain enough. For in my opinion, they were.

FOOTNOTES:

Introduction:

1. Hitchens, p. xviii

Part One:

1. http://www.olympic.org/news/london-2012-provides-many-magical-moments/172475
2. Lee, p. 179
3. Lewis, Leo - The Times; 31 May 2014, page 32.
4. Ibid
5. Ibid
6. Ibid
7. Ibid
8. "The Washington Journal"; Washington DC, BBC Parliament - 15 February 2015
9. Ibid
10. http://www.respectparty.org/2015/03/15/senior-labour-figure-defects-to-respect/
11. Horne & Whannel, p. 28
12. Hansard; 5 February 2014, Column 265
13. Lee, p. 87
14. Horne & Whannel, p. 92
15. The 1924 British Empire Exhibition, at Wembley, London, April-October: handbook of general information, in Horne & Whannel ed. p. 97

16. Horne & Whannel, p. 98

17. Ibid

18. Jones in Horne & Whannel ed., pp. 196-7

19. Horne & Whannel, p. 140

20. Horne & Whannel, p. 139

21. Lee, p. 170

22. Lee, p. 25

23. Ennis, p. 68

Part Two:

1. Horne & Whannel, p. 69

2. Ibid

3. Hill, Amelia - The Guardian; 7 January 2001.

4. "In 1990, half of the white population disapproved of racially mixed relationships. Now, according to a new survey by the think-tank British Futures, only around 15 per cent mind" - Alibhai-Brown, Yasmin – The Independent; 9 December 2012.

5. Rogan & Rogan, p. 71

6. Horne & Whannel, p. 79

7. Carlin, John - Observer Sports Monthly; May 2002 edition, page 46.

8. Ibid

9. In spite of his historical ethics in coining Olympism, de Coubertin did not like women taking part.

10. Horne & Whannel, p. 105

11. Rogan & Rogan p. 15

12. Horne & Whannel, p. 150
13. Marx in Horne & Whannel ed. p. 183

Part Three:

1. Lee, p. 85
2. Lee, pp. 179-80
3. Lee, p. 39
4. Lee, p. 173
5. Lee, p. 178
6. Lee, p. 177
7. Horne & Whannel, p. 104
8. Spink
9. Ibid
10. Ibid
11. Ibid
12. Horne & Whannel, p. 181
13. Jones in Horne & Whannel ed., pp. 196-7
14. Rogan & Rogan, p. 86
15. Lee, p. 178
16. Horne & Whannel, p. 98
17. The Daily Telegraph; 28 July 2012
18. The Independent (Online article), 30 July 2012
19. The Daily Telegraph; 28 July 2012
20. Ibid
21. The Guardian (Online article); 30 July 2012
22. "London 2012: Closing Ceremony"; London, BBC One – 12 August 2012
23. Ibid

Conclusion:

1. Hilton, p. 11
2. Lee, p. 180
3. Hilton, p. 13
4. Alibhai-Brown, Yasmin - The Independent; 9 December 2012
5. "Question Time"; Newport, BBC One – 27 February 2014
6. Carrington in Horne & Whannel ed., p. 167
7. Ibid
8. Ibid
9. Lee, p. 48
10. Hansard; 24 June 2015, Column 981
11. Horne & Whannel, p. 31
12. Ibid
13. Rogan & Rogan p. 3

BIBLIOGRAPHY:

Carlin, John.

"There's no pleasure for Argentines quite like beating the country that taught them how to play"
The Observer Sport Monthly, May 2002.
Page 46.

Carrington, Ben.

Cosmopolitan Olympism, Humanism and the Spectacle of "Race". (2004), in John Horne & Garry Whannel ed. Understanding the Olympics

Ennis, Jessica.

Unbelievable: From my Childhood Dreams to Winning Olympic Gold.
(London: Hodder & Stoughton, 2012)

Hilton, Christopher.

Hitler's Olympics: The 1936 Berlin Olympic Games
(Stroud: Sutton, 2006)

Hitchens, Peter.

The Abolition of Britain
(London: Quartet, 1999)

Horne, John & Whannel, Garry.

Understanding the Olympics
(Oxford: Routledge, 2011)

Jones, Paul.

The Sociology of Architecture and the Politics of Building (2006), in John Horne & Garry Whannel ed. Understanding the Olympics

Lee, Mike.

The Race for the 2012 Olympics
(London: Virgin, 2006)

Marx, Karl.

Das Kapital (1867)
in John Horne & Garry Whannel ed. Understanding the Olympics

Rippon, Anton.

Hitler's Olympics: The Story of the 1936 Nazi Games (Barnsley: Pen & Sword, 2012)

Roche, Maurice.

Mega Events and Modernity: Olympics and Expos in the Growth of Global Culture (2000), in John Horne & Garry Whannel ed. Understanding the Olympics

Rogan, Martin & Rogan, Matt.

Britain and the Olympic Games: Past, Present, Legacy (Leicester: Matador, 2011)

WEBOGRAPHY:

Alibhai-Brown, Yasmin.

"Whether she wins Sports Personality of the Year or not, Jessica Ennis represents the best of Britain"
(December 9 2012;
http://www.independent.co.uk/voices/comment/whethe
r-she-wins-sports-personality-of-the-year-or-not-
jessica-ennis-represents-the-best-of-britain-
8397346.html)

Hill, Amelia.

"Dyke: BBC is hideously white"
(January 7 2001,
http://www.theguardian.com/media/2001/jan/07/uknew
s.theobserver1)

Spink, Sheila.

"Party Pooper – Is the Russian President sending a message to the rest of the world?"
(February 10 2014,
http://www.bnp.org.uk/news/national/party-pooper-
russian-president-sending-message-western-world)

ABOUT THE AUTHOR

Born in Surrey, John Moore grew up in Farnborough on the county's border with Hampshire in southern England. He attended both preparatory and comprehensive school, before garnering qualifications at his local college in both Media Studies and the French language prior to attending university in Southampton. He has tried his hand at film criticism, something which has previously resulted in a number of his reviews being published in a local magazine; worked as a volunteer for a foodbank charity and enjoys the game of chess. He resides on the south coast of England.